Personal and Social Education in the Curriculum

Studies in Teaching and Learning
General Editor
Denis Lawton, B.A., Ph.D.
Professor of Education and Director,
University of London Institute of Education

In the series:

Denis Lawton *An Introduction to Teaching and Learning*
John Robertson *Effective Classroom Control*
Maurice Holt *Evaluating the Evaluators*
Richard Aldrich *An Introduction to the History of Education*
Edwin Cox *Problems and Possibilities for Religious Education*
Denis Lawton *Curriculum Studies and Educational Planning*
Richard Pring *Personal and Social Education in the Curriculum*
Malcolm Skilbeck (ed.) *Evaluating the Curriculum in the Eighties*
Jagdish S. Gundara, Crispin Jones and Keith Kimberley (eds) *Education in a Multicultural Society*
Patrick D. Walsh *Values in Teaching and Learning*
Maggie Ing *Psychology, Teaching and Learning*

Personal and Social Education in the Curriculum

Concepts and Content

Richard Pring

HODDER AND STOUGHTON
LONDON SYDNEY AUCKLAND TORONTO

to Helen

British Library Cataloguing in Publication Data

Pring, Richard
Personal and social education in the curriculum.—
(Studies in teaching and learning)
1. Moral education
I. Title   II. Series
370.11′4   LC268

ISBN 0 340 33422 3

First published 1984

Printed and bound in Great Britain for
Hodder and Stoughton Educational,
a division of Hodder and Stoughton Ltd,
Mill Road, Dunton Green, Sevenoaks, Kent,
by Biddles Ltd, Guildford, Surrey

Typeset in 11 on 12 pt Plantin (Linotron) by
Rowland Phototypesetting Ltd
Bury St Edmunds, Suffolk

Contents

Acknowledgments

I should like to thank:
Sue Newall who has so carefully and quickly prepared the manuscript; Denis Lawton who prompted and encouraged me to write the book and whose comments on the early draft were so very helpful; David Evans and John Thacker, Olwen Goodall and Pam Stoate, colleagues at the University of Exeter School of Education, upon whose work, conversations, and criticisms I have liberally drawn; MOSAIC (in particular Helen Weinreich-Haste, Peter Kutnik, David Evans, Derek Wright) whose seminars over several years have provided an invaluable background; CIRCE, University of Illinois College of Education, in particular its director Bob Stake who provided the excellent facilities, good company and abundant ice cream essential for writing a book; Faye for her support and criticism, and Helen, Katherine and Sally for providing the examples.

Studies in Teaching and Learning

The purpose of this series of short books on education is to make available readable, up-to-date views on educational issues and controversies. Its aim will be to provide teachers and students (and perhaps parents and governors) with a series of books which will introduce those educational topics which any intelligent and professional educationist ought to be familiar with. One of the criticisms levelled against 'teacher-education' is that there is so little agreement about what ground should be covered in courses at various levels; one assumption behind this series of texts is that there is a common core of knowledge and skills that all teachers need to be aware of, and the series is designed to map out this territory.

Although the major intention of the series is to provide general coverage, each volume will consist of more than a review of the relevant literature; the individual authors will be encouraged to give their own personal interpretation of the field and the way it is developing.

Introduction

A principal of an American high school sends this letter to his teachers on the first day of school.

> *Dear Teacher*
> *I am a survivor of a concentration camp. My eyes saw what no man should witness:*
> *Gas chambers built by learned engineers.*
> *Children poisoned by educated physicians.*
> *Infants killed by trained nurses.*
> *Women and babies shot and burned by high school and college graduates.*
> *So, I am suspicious of education.*
> *My request is: Help your students become human. Your efforts must never produce learned monsters, skilled psychopaths, educated Eichmans.*
> *Reading, writing, arithmetic are important only if they serve to make our children more human.*

(See Strom, 1981, page 4 and chapter 6 of this book, section 2.)

Note

I have adopted the policy of randomly using 'he' or 'she'. The reason is that that seemed the most impartial thing to do in a book that ought to be fairly self-conscious about the different influences on personal development.

Richard Pring

PART I

Concepts

1 Identifying the Problem

1 Setting the Scene

Schools have always been concerned with personal and social development. Teachers give moral instruction and advice. Pupils explore personal and moral issues through literature. Teachers show care for children's welfare beyond their teaching duties. Often this concern is implicit in the ethos and 'way of life' of the school – the rules to be followed or the relationships fostered between teacher and pupils. Personal and social development, however, can be part of the curriculum more directly through tutorial periods and other aspects of the pastoral system of the school – or, indeed, through the treatment of topics in the humanities, religious education, or social studies. Any subjects (as in literature) or activities (as with community projects) that confront personal, social, or moral values, may contribute to personal and social development.

Recently, however, various reports have expressed the view that personal and social development needs a more central and explicit place in the curriculum. For example, the DES/HMI (1980) report, *A View of the Curriculum*, declares that

> . . . personal and social development in this broad sense ['. . . prepared to meet the basic intellectual and social demands of adult life, and helped to form an acceptable set of personal values . . .'] is a major charge on the curriculum.
>
> (page 2)

This follows the HMI surveys of what is happening in primary and secondary schools. The opening lines of the chapter in the secondary survey (DES/HMI, 1979) which was devoted entirely to personal and social development says that:

In recent years, these major objectives [namely, 'opportunities and experiences . . . that will help their personal development as well as preparing them for the next stage of their lives'] have assumed a more significant and conscious place in the aspirations of schools in response to external pressures and to changes in society, and within the schools themselves.

(page 206)

In concluding the curriculum section of this chapter, HMI indicates the wide front on which these objectives must be pursued.

It is clear that there is a need for many schools to reconsider curricula, methods of teaching, use of resources and methods of grouping pupils with regard to their impact on pupils' personal development.

(page 218)

Other reports, too, have taken up the theme – the DES (1977) consultative document *Education in Schools* which sets out the major aims of education, the DES (1979) and (1981) papers, *A Framework for the Curriculum* and *The School Curriculum* respectively, which translate these aims into objectives, and the Schools Council (1981) report *The Practical Curriculum*. Furthermore, attempts to map out the major areas of the curriculum picked out the ethical and the social, or personal and social development, as major areas (for example, the DES/HMI, 1977, report *Curriculum 11 to 16* and the APU[1] framework as described by Kay, 1975). And in the most significant educational developments since 1944, namely the changes in the provision and curriculum for fourteen to nineteen year olds, a central place is provided for social and life skills, moral values, and sense of responsibility (see FEU,[2] 1979 and 1980a, MSC,[3] 1980). In the light of these recommendations, local education authorities (LEA) are producing reports on personal and social development (see, for example, Devon County Council, 1982) and appointments of teachers are being made to schools with this specific responsibility. Indeed, the very forward looking consultative document of Coventry LEA is an excellent example of how some educational planners see programmes of personal and social education, with appropriate training of teachers, to be central to educational planning if provision is to meet both individual pupils' and the local community's needs in the years ahead (see Coventry Education Committee, 1982).

2 Problems

It remains unclear, however, how this general concern can be translated into curriculum practice. There are five kinds of problem.

(a) Conceptual

Personal and social development covers so many different aspects of a pupil's development that it seems impossible to make any coherent sense of it as a curriculum area. Confining our attention for the moment solely to the reports already referred to, we have: forming 'an acceptable set of personal values', 'moral attitudes' (not specified in detail), 'capacity to participate actively within society and to contribute responsibly to it', 'social competence', 'skills of good personal relationships', 'spiritual awareness', 'careers guidance', 'living and working together amicably', 'capacity to exercise leadership', 'self-esteem and self-confidence', 'respect for animals', 'appropriate attitudes towards sex, parenthood, smoking, drink and exercise' – the list is apparently endless. Personal and social development, though sounding grand, seems to be no more than a pot-pourri of sweet sounding, but only loosely connected, skills, habits, bits of knowledge, attitudes, behaviours, feelings. Furthermore, selection from all these would seem to reflect no more than what this or that teacher thinks to be personally nice and socially useful.

The conceptual problems are of various kinds. Sometimes the development refers to skills (the social and life skills examined by the FEU), sometimes to personal qualities or virtues such as tolerance or kindness, sometimes to specific bits of knowledge, sometimes to ways of behaving. And yet the connection is unclear between knowledge and understanding (the cognitive), feelings, attitudes, and qualities of character (the affective), and how people behave.

Furthermore once this complex analysis of personal development is applied to the wide range of social contexts in which the adolescent or young school leaver must live – the contexts of employment (or indeed of unemployment), of raising a family, of sexual relationships, of political involvement – the area seems too vast and amorphous for coherent analysis and for formulating clear curriculum policies. Better to stick to the well-trodden paths of traditional subjects.

(b) Political

Personal and social development cannot avoid political questions however 'neutral' the teacher's role is considered to be. It is concerned with the quality of personal life certainly, but the quality of that life depends upon the sort of society one lives in and upon the social relationships created thereby. On the other hand, the type of society we live in will depend upon the personal qualities developed in young people. It is, needless to say, a two-way process: individuals affecting social values and relationships, and society in turn shaping the personal values, habits, and understanding of each individual. Those who accept responsibility for the personal and social development of young people inevitably raise questions about the sort of society children are developing into, and must sometimes accept a clash between the personal qualities and attitudes they wish to foster within home and classroom and the social standards prevailing elsewhere.

There is a particular difficulty here reflected in the official documents referred to which, separately, emphasise quite different aspects of personal and social development. Some reports stress preparation for adult responsibilities (those of the voter, the parent, the worker) and the relation of school to work. Others give particular attention to promoting moral and personal qualities – moral reasoning, awareness of one's own values and attitudes, self-esteem and human dignity, respect for and tolerance of others, independence of thought. Generally speaking, the stress upon preparation for working life, with an emphasis upon careers guidance and industrial experience, is characteristic more of the documents written by DES officials than of HMI reports. But the DES/HMI (1977) paper *Curriculum 11 to 16* is aware of the possible difficulty:

> . . . the educational system is charged by society . . . with equipping young people to take their place as citizens and workers in adult life . . . Secondly there is the responsibility for educating the 'autonomous citizen', a person able to think and act for herself or himself, to resist exploitation, to innovate and to be vigilant in the defence of liberty. These two functions do not always fit easily together.

(page 9)

Put briefly, the schools cannot ignore the *sort* of persons that they are trying to produce, and 'sort of person' will need to be spelt out in reference to, on the one hand, personal qualities that we think desirable and, on the other, wider social needs. And, unless one is careful, the two might conflict.

(c) Ethical

Personal and social development raises questions not only about the sort of society one wishes to foster and encourage but also about the sort of person one wishes to live within that society. Which qualities are to count as virtues (thus to be developed) and which as vices? Values permeate the whole of personal and social education, and moral development is at the centre. There is, however, the prevailing view that values are ultimately a matter of taste or are relative to particular social conditions, and that teachers have no right to promote one set of values rather than another. Teachers are soon accused of indoctrination, and that seems to be the ultimate sin.

It is argued therefore in several of the reports that pupils should be helped to form their own stable set of personal values rather than be told what they are. And, consistent with such a view, there has been a growth, particularly in North America, of 'values clarification' as a way of helping pupils to do this.

In my view such a position is mistaken and one can list a range of qualities which seem good bets in any recognisable moral form of life and which would receive fairly universal agreement – not hurting people for the sheer delight of it, keeping promises, not cooking the books. Even where there is within society such disagreement that teachers, whatever their personal views, feel disqualified from promoting a particular moral line (for example, in certain instances of sexual relationships), there could still be agreement on principles for guiding personal choice, such as respecting other persons' wishes or not exploiting their weaknesses. This I shall argue later. But any attempt to make sense of personal and social development cannot avoid listing the personal values or principles of behaviour that should be part of that development, and this, given the difficulties of ethical argument, will necessarily be controversial.

(d) Empirical

There is little reliable empirical evidence upon which to base any thoroughgoing programme of personal and social development.

The problems of empirical investigation are of course tied up with the conceptual, political and value problems referred to above, as we shall see. But there are deeper theoretical issues at stake here, for what counts as evidence for a particular conclusion will depend upon the perspective adopted. Those, for instance, who put a lot of faith in techniques of behaviour modification (see chapter 4, section 2) interpret the behavioural evidence in a particular way. They make assumptions about motivation and behaviour which are at variance with the assumptions of those whom I, for the moment, shall call the 'cognitive developmentalists'. They 'see' things differently and in order therefore to reconcile the differences you need not simply to look for new facts but also to examine the concepts and ideas through which those 'facts' are seen and interpreted.

There are, however, more obvious difficulties in getting empirical backing for a particular policy on personal or social development. People are very complex 'things' and their development takes place over many years. It is never possible to capture the enormous range of experiences or physical or social conditions that might have affected the way in which people develop. Nor is it morally possible to treat them experimentally, controlling certain elements in their environment whilst changing and examining others. Above all, as *persons* they have an inner life of their own, reacting thoughtfully and actively to these various influences. We are not therefore in the province of carefully controlled experiments with objects that can be manipulated.

(e) Organisational

The secondary school curriculum is organised around subjects, and teachers are appointed, for the most part, to teach these subjects. It is a constant complaint that there is not enough room on the timetable for yet further subjects or content. How then, it is asked, can attention be given to personal and social development? The problem is clearly less acute in primary schools, but even there it is not clear what place personal and social development should have alongside the basic skills, the projects and the arts which constitute the curriculum.

3   This Book

The five problems listed in section 2 enter into our educational thinking in planning the curriculum (what and how to teach) and in giving an account of what has been achieved. It is not possible to engage in curriculum planning, or to be held accountable to a wider public, where there is little agreement over what is being aimed at, where the same words mean so many different things, or where the values which the school serves are regarded as essentially a private or personal matter. And yet most people – teachers, parents, employers, or the community at large – intuitively believe that there is something to be picked out by what is referred to as personal and social development and that schools have a responsibility for promoting it.

The difficulties are to some extent philosophical. In clarifying ideas on personal and social development for curriculum purposes, one is quickly into issues about which philosophers have had a lot to say – for example, what it is to be a person, the respective places of 'learning' and 'development' in becoming a person, the rationality or otherwise of adopting a set of values, the relation of personal rights and responsibilities to the social good. Not to see these problems for what they are – the subject matter at a certain level of analysis, of ethics, of the philosophy of mind, of political and social philosophy – would be to trivialise them, and ultimately to trivialise the curriculum thinking in this area.

This book therefore aims to do several things. Firstly, it 'maps out' the territory to see whether, beneath the many different and at times competing claims falling under personal and social development, some coherent sense can be made of it as a curriculum area. To do this chapter 2 examines what it means to be a 'person' and what therefore is involved in personal development. Chapter 3 then considers the contribution made to the understanding of personal development by certain social psychologists. This provides a central strand and theoretical perspective amid the bewildering detail. But it is necessary, in order to meet some of the difficulties already referred to, to return in chapter 4 to a more philosophical examination of the moral language through which we understand the personal lives of ourselves and other people.

Secondly, chapter 5 onwards translates all this into curriculum terms, with sufficient detail to enable schools to examine their own provision and to raise relevant questions about practice.

Thirdly, practical suggestions of what might be tried out in the classroom are provided throughout. But there are limits upon how useful this can be because of differences in classroom circumstances, in teaching styles and relationships, in moral and political climate, and in children's backgrounds.

It must not be forgotten however that, whatever our immediate practical concerns, our interest in personal and social development raises fundamental questions about the purposes and effectiveness of schooling which should never be too far from our minds. Can schools seriously affect the attitudes and behaviour of young people towards society and towards one another? Should schools accept this responsibility amongst their many others? If so what sort of society, informed by what civic and political values, should schools be helping to form? What sort of personal values and habits should teachers be encouraging in young people and indeed by what authority? These are highly charged moral and professional and indeed political questions, but some answers to them are necessary if schools are to be encouraged to help with the personal and social development of children.

NOTES

1 APU The Assessment of Performance Unit was established within the Department of Education and Science (DES) in 1974. Although initially it was presented as a means of testing disadvantaged children in order to diagnose their special difficulties, its main aim soon became that of monitoring pupil performance across the curriculum at different ages. To achieve this it needed a curriculum model. It picked out seven areas of development which, it was argued, represented all that went on within the curriculum – mathematical, scientific, language, aesthetic, physical, personal and social, and foreign language development. In 1979, however, it was decided not to proceed with monitoring pupil performance in the area of personal and social development. See Pring (1980) for a critical account of this model with special reference to the personal and social development area.

2 FEU The Further Education Unit is an advisory, intelligence and development body for further education. It was established in 1977 by the Secretary of State for Education and Science to make possible a more co-ordinated and cohesive approach to curriculum development in further education. It has concentrated in particular upon prevocational developments, that is, those post-16 courses which do

not lead to a job-specific qualification but which are oriented towards broad areas of employment. In *A Basis for Choice* (1979), the FEU recommended criteria that should govern the development of such courses. One important feature of its recommendation was its 'common core curriculum' which was translated into twelve broad aims, each broken down into more specific learning objectives and worthwhile experiences. Aim 4 was 'to bring about an ability to develop satisfactory personal relationships with others'. Aim 5 was 'to provide a basis on which the young person acquires a set of moral values applicable to issues in contemporary society'. *A Basis for Choice* has been very influential in the proposals for the new 17+ Certificate of Prevocational Education (CPVE) and the development of City and Guilds of London Institute course 365, Vocational Preparation (General), which many young people at school and college are taking.

3   MSC   The Manpower Services Commission is a unit established under the Department of Employment aimed at reviewing and improving the preparation of people for the country's economic and industrial needs. Under its New Training Initiative (announced by the Department of Employment in 1981 in its White Paper, *A New Training Initiative: a programme for action* and based on the MSC's own 1981 paper, *A New Training Initiative: an agenda for action*) it has three main tasks: (1) to develop skill training, with special reference to a reform of the apprenticeship system; (2) to widen opportunities for adults; (3) to equip all young people for work. In pursuit of the third objective, the MSC has guaranteed planned work experience and work-related training and education to all young school leavers from September 1983 onwards. This is known as the Youth Training Scheme (YTS). The joint statement of the MSC and FEU describes some of the agreed principles concerning the training and education of young people.

(a)   The creation of a coherent programme of vocational preparation for all young people should be given a high priority both by the training and education sector.

(b)   Vocational preparation programmes, however based, should conform to broad national guidelines amenable to local implementation to suit the needs of employers and of the young people themselves.

(c)   Such programmes should have common aims related to the acquisition of skill, experience and knowledge; the optimisation of employability; an understanding of the adult world; experience of work; a progressive approach to the responsibility for self development and a willingness to accept change.

(d)   The five main elements described in paragraph twenty six of the Government White Paper are generally recommended. Briefly these were
　　　(i)   Induction and assessment;

    (ii)   Basic skills;
    (iii) Occupationally relevant education and training;
    (iv) Guidance and counselling;
    (v)   Record and review of progress.

There is a constant stress in reports upon social and life skills as part of this vocational preparation since these (broadly understood) seem essential to 'employability' and to 'the responsibility for self development and a willingness to accept change'.

More recently the MSC has supported work in schools as part of its Technical and Vocational Education Initiative (TVEI, see page 111, Note 2) – a scheme to encourage coherent educational programmes from fourteen to eighteen which incorporate a greater vocational and technical orientation than is traditionally the case.

2   Being a Person

1   Education and 'Personhood'

Teachers exercise control over children. Being *in* control, they *do* things to them and change them in ways that they, the teachers, want. Teachers, therefore, make assumptions about the appropriate ends of children's development and also about the morally acceptable means of achieving those ends. But how teachers treat children and what they judge to be appropriate goals of their development depend upon what sort of 'things' they see young people to be. How you treat people depends upon your concept of 'person'. It is necessary, therefore, to sort out first what it means to be a person and then what the connections are between the 'development of persons' and educating them.

Firstly, a person is an object that you can see, touch, and smell, that you can push, measure, and weigh. In that respect a person is like any other physical object, and can be made to do things and be manipulated accordingly.

Secondly, however, the objects picked out by the concept 'person' have qualities or capacities which cannot be exhaustively spelt out in terms of those attributes associated with physical objects as such. Persons, but not stones, have a form of consciousness. To be conscious of things requires some set of concepts through which experience is ordered and made sense of.

Thirdly, the objects (that is human beings) picked out by the concept of person are not conscious of things in a purely passive sense – like a camera receiving snapshots of the world outside. Rather do they react with that world in a *purposeful* way, attributing meaning to particular events, anticipating what is to happen, and changing the course of action accordingly. We attribute to persons, therefore, *intentionality* and we typically explain their behaviour in terms, not of causes, but of intentions and of motives.

The intentionality of persons is picked out by a wide range of mental concepts that we need for giving an account of people, such as 'willing', 'trying', 'hoping', 'regretting'.

Fourthly, that form of consciousness through which a person makes sense of the world must itself contain the concept of person. Without it a person would not be able to deal with the world as it is, namely, as a world that contains not only physical objects but persons as I have described them, or be able to relate to other persons in a 'person-like way'. A necessary part of living a human form of life is that people communicate with each other and thus relate, not simply as physical objects do in a purely causal sense, but in a meaningful way. I can talk to people because I see them as something more than flesh and blood, as having ideas and intentions. I try to understand them, not simply manipulate them. Of course, in having a concept of a person I can see not only other people as persons but also myself. Self-reflection in some degree seems to be a feature of being a person.

Fifthly, 'persons' picks out objects that not only have a form of conscious life and engage in purposeful activities but also possess moral attributes. We say not only that a person thought or did something, but that he was in some way responsible for what he did and we praise or blame him accordingly and we ascribe certain rights and obligations. Obviously the possibility of such moral appraisals is closely connected with the possibility of intentional behaviour and of acting from motives. Such moral appraisals do seem to be an indispensable part of our relationships with other persons in which some element of trust, honesty, and concern seems to be necessary.

A strong connection between becoming a person and education in this sense is made by Langford (1973). In his essay 'The Concept of Education', he argues that 'to become educated is to learn to be a person'. This, on the surface, appears simply wrong. Are, then, babies not persons? No doubt Langford would agree that he is stipulating a definition which is not altogether in tune with how we ordinarily use these words. But his claim does underline some important conceptual truths that we are in danger of forgetting. We can for instance, and indeed often do, make a distinction between being a person and being *merely* a man (a member of the biological species). People with very severe brain damage may be thought of as vegetables, not persons. A foetus, even when properly formed as a member of the biological species of man, would be regarded by some as not yet a person (and presumably able to be aborted without the indictment of murder).

Furthermore, the distinction is frequently implicit in attitudes adopted towards individuals or groups of people. People from different races have in the past sometimes been treated as non-persons – not having those qualities which make someone a person, and thus to be classed for moral purposes as little better than animals, or, as in the case of slaves, as bits of property. Or, again, different attitudes are shown towards different categories of people (grown-ups as opposed to babies, the healthy as opposed to the mentally defective, the worthy as opposed to the depraved) where these differences could be explained in terms of respect for some, but not for others, as having become persons.

There does therefore seem to be a strong case for saying, first, that one can distinguish between being a human being (a member of the biological species) and being a person; that, secondly, the qualities that transform a human being into being a person need to be acquired and then to be developed; and that, thirdly, the ability to extend the notion to others can be more or less limited, and frequently open to improvement. *Becoming* a person would lie in the gradual acquisition of those capacities to think, feel, and believe which seem essential to being a person.

Such powers of thought and feeling and action do develop relatively early, however, and to that extent, in some minimal but recognisable sense, a baby become a person during its very early months. If this is so, then the identification of education with *becoming* a person is too strong a way of expressing an important truth. Persons *are* the 'things' that you educate. Education is a matter, not of turning non-persons into persons, but rather of helping people to become more fully persons – that is, to acquire in a more complete way those powers of reasoning, feeling, and acting responsibly which distinguish someone as a person and which, as a very young child, he or she possesses in a minimal and undeveloped way.

The close connection that Langford makes between becoming a person (or, as I would argue, more fully a person) and 'education' might be approached from a different angle. There is a tendency, in some of the documents referred to, to treat education as a 'thing' or as a package of things that one acquires or attends or simply swallows as a means to some further end. 'Education' gets you a job or enables you to be useful to society or is important for keeping industry going or is the means for creating a more equal society. It is like a commodity that can be bought and sold, distributed equally or unequally, used or not for personal advantage.

'Education' can have this meaning. We do refer to a person's education as though simply a package of things that happened to him or a set of institutions that he attended or a collection of certificates and qualifications he received. And 'education' so understood is frequently evaluated in terms of what can be got from it. There is, however, a different sense of 'education' that the reference to personal development brings out. We can do things to children certainly, and enable them subsequently to do what is required of them. But it remains unclear why this is necessarily part of a person's *education* because it is unclear why it touches him *as a person*. Personal development as an educational aim does at least force us to attend to certain features of being a person which can so easily get lost in the more utilitarian aims of the educational system.[1]

Such attention to what it is to be a person is not incompatible with a view of schooling as providing socially useful skills. But it is possible to distinguish between skills, knowledge, understanding which, although socially useful, fail to affect that person in any central way, and those mental and physical attainments that seem central to this or that child's development as a person. I may learn to calculate, to use a protractor, to play a tune on the piano, or to recite a poem, but remain much the same *person* – discarding these bits of knowledge or skill when the occasion no longer demands. I may be well trained in such things and I may be able to apply such training to socially useful tasks when called upon to do so. But the 'I' which does these things remains in some sense unaffected.

On the other hand I may acquire these skills and understandings in a 'significant way', altering thereby the understanding and the valuings I have of myself, of other people with whom I interact, or of the physical conditions in which I live, and altering thereby my power and motivation to change myself and the world in which I live. The aim of personal development does therefore draw our attention to central educational concern for how pupils see and value themselves, others, and the world around them.

These points might be summarised in the following way. We are told that the curriculum should aim at, amongst other things, personal development. This can be interpreted in three ways at least. It should aim at helping pupils (i) to become persons, or (ii) to develop as persons, that is to become persons in a fuller sense, or

(iii) to develop important personal qualities. With reference to (i), namely becoming persons, then if 'persons' is to be understood in the sense suggested by Langford, a child is a person as soon as he or she has some form of conceptual life and self-determined action, and this will have been achieved long before formal education has begun. With reference to (ii), namely developing as persons, then we need to identify those powers and qualities which are definitive of being a person but which are in need of development. With reference to (iii), namely developing important personal qualities, then we need to specify what *sort* of person we want to produce as a result of our educational endeavour – the qualities that we value most about people but which at the same time are not central to being a person.

I want to argue that personal and social development requires a bit of both (ii) and (iii) and that there is something in the notion of being 'more fully a person' or 'more of a person', and not just being a person of a certain sort, which programmes of personal development must take into account.

2   Developing as a Person

To develop *as* a person is to acquire the ways of understanding and of behaving which pick out objects as persons and which are only potentially or minimally present in the young child.

In the first section above I picked out the capacity to see oneself and others as persons to be an essential characteristic of being a person. You cannot relate to someone *as a person* unless you have the concept of person and are able to apply it. What we do know however is that this concept, and thus the sort of relationships one is able to have, only gradually emerges. Let us examine this briefly.

Part of the early growth of awareness lies in gradually distinguishing material objects as such from persons. Persons may have bodies and be knocked around like other bits of matter, but they are something else besides. They have feelings, and thoughts, and they do things intentionally. One can attribute to them motives, dispositions and character traits. Moreover, just as I can perceive them as having these attributes, I can also perceive them as perceiving me having them too. I gradually become aware, in other words, not simply of others having certain mental qualities but of myself as having these qualities, and of others, by reason of these qualities, standing in certain kinds of relationships to me. Such a form of awareness and of personal relationship begins to emerge at a very young age. Indeed, a baby soon engages in an elementary form of personal relationship, sharing or reciprocating such feelings as anger or affection or resentment, anticipating the grown-ups' behaviour, and communicating at a fairly basic level. A certain reciprocity is soon apparent. Bruner (1975), for example, demonstrates how very early indeed there are indications that the baby communicates with and recognises the intentions of the mother, and that such 'mutuality' is the essential starting point for the learning of language. In practice therefore the young child has a concept of a person in some minimal sense as is reflected in the personal relationships he has with his mother and father. To that extent he sees them as persons. Indeed some would argue that the perception of objects as persons is prior to the perception of objects *simpliciter*, and that it is only gradually that the distinction comes to be made between persons and non persons. 'Animism' is a characteristic of early childhood well described by Piaget.

This early ability, however, to pick objects out as persons, and to relate to them as such, is itself in need of development. Only gradually does the young child come to see the full implications of her growing awareness that others, too, can think and feel and have intentions. It is this growing consciousness of what is implied in a *personal* relationship with others which constitutes an important part of development as a person. Furthermore, since this knowledge of other persons is intimately connected with how one relates to them even as an infant, so the development as a person will be closely connected with the sort of personal relationships one is able to enjoy. It is therefore important for those concerned with the personal development of children to describe this growing consciousness in greater detail, to show how it might be assessed at different stages, and to give some account of how it comes about and how it might be enhanced by training or teaching.

There are several ways in which seeing others as persons, and thereby relating to them as persons, can be said to develop. Firstly, although a young child shows through her behaviour that she recognises others as having mental attributes such as intentions and emotions, she does not realise at first that such intentions and feelings might be different from her own (Flavell, 1974). Only gradually, as any reflective parent knows, does the child become aware that the other's 'inner life' is not, in any particular situation, exactly like one's own. Even though I am feeling lively, the other person might be feeling tired, and although I need to *learn* how to recognise the signs of different mental states, this learning requires the prior ability to distinguish between one's own state of mind and that of other people. It is the absence of this ability which Piaget (1926) refers to as ego-centrism, and of course, as in any changing psychological capacity, the transition from ego-centrism to altruism is a gradual one.

Secondly, one can have the concept of person but, through lack of imagination or through not having grasped it fully, fail to apply it as widely as one might. Different periods of history show how the concept of person was not applied to particular people – to blacks, or to heathens, or to slaves, or to women, or to children. It was as though they lacked certain attributes – the capacity to think or to reflect or to act responsibly – which are essential for personhood. But failure of the imagination may not be confined to such instances. One can be capable of inferring someone else's mental state, but not have the habit or tendency to do so. For some it requires a conscious effort to realise that others may not see things as one does oneself, and frequently communication breaks down, even between teacher and pupil, through the failure to grasp this very fact.

Thirdly, however, connected with this developing sophistication of personal understanding is a qualitative change in the sort of relationships that one person can have with another. Such development is briefly mapped out by Peters (1974a). In the very early years ('pre-rational' and then 'ego-centric') the child might not recognise that others see things differently from herself. People are appraised in self-referential terms, and the child therefore relates to them in a rather instrumental way. Only later does she reach the stage of what Peters calls 'realism' in which others can be seen to play different roles (that of policeman, of teacher) and thereby to have distinctive points of view. Consequently, she is able to relate to them as holding certain kinds of position or as fulfilling certain roles. Only later still (the stage of autonomy) does she come to recognise the individuality of a person's point of view – what the other has worked out for him or herself. There is then the possibility of relating to someone not in an instrumental way or indeed as the reflection of a certain type of character or role, but as a unique individual.

Peters' account of the growing perception of other people as persons and thus of the sort of relationships one can have with other people is similar in many respects to the account given by Secord and Peevers (1974). This study, arising from an analysis of the ways in which children in particular situations describe others and attribute certain mental qualities to them, maps out the developing understanding of others and then themselves as persons. Initially others are known simply by reference to the situation they are in (for example, the man who lives in that street), and later by individual characteristics. Only later still do such individual characteristics become 'personal', that is refer to specific interests, abilities, or beliefs, and finally to dispositions that characterise the person in question (for example, lazy or cruel). The distinction therefore between intention and motive in explaining someone's behaviour becomes clear only relatively later – 'he acted out of jealousy or ambition' – and with it the clear sense of a person being responsible for what he did, of being praised or blameworthy, and of having or not having self-control.

One can therefore make some sense of the notion of developing as a person in so far as there is evidence that the sort of consciousness which is characteristic of being a person, although present in some elementary form at a very early age, only gradually emerges. Furthermore, since the nature of this consciousness enters into the relationships one forms with others, so there emerges the capacity for different kinds of personal relationships – from the rather ego-centric and instrumental of the young child to the close personal relationship that one gets in love or close friendships.

Here I have done no more than to try to make sense of the notion. In the next chapter I shall show how, through recent work in social psychology, the notion of 'development as a person' might be worked out in much greater detail in a way that is relevant to both teachers and parents. However, there is one aspect of this development which I have touched upon but which needs to be explained more fully. Persons, as I explained earlier, do things in the light of their knowledge and understanding, and in return they are held responsible for what they do, and are praised or blamed accordingly. It is a matter of common sense however that there are degrees to which a person can be held responsible. In law, people sometimes plead not guilty or are excused the full penalty of their crime because of diminished responsibility or extenuating circumstances. Even more so is it the case with young children. Only gradually are we prepared to ascribe full responsibility for their actions, and for determining their own future. To be responsible for what one does and for one's own destiny is part of what we mean by being a person but this is only slowly achieved, and some, one might observe, achieve it to only a small degree. Their lives are characterised by irresponsibility, or by a reluctance to take on the burdens of deciding their actions, and they remain dependent on the decisions of other people.

This is a difficult notion to sort out in detail. But it underlies the frequent reference to 'autonomy' as an educational ideal and as the proper end of personal development (see Dearden, 1972). By autonomy is meant self-determination or control over one's own life and decisions. It is contrasted with the situation in which someone is not master of his own situation, but whose life is the product of influences or forces or desires or emotions over which he has little control. Since autonomy has had such an important place in recent accounts of personal development, I shall return to it in chapter 4.

Meanwhile, to summarise this rather difficult section I reiterate the following points. First, we can talk of development *as* a person in so far as those qualities which seem essential to being a person and which exist only potentially or minimally in the very young child do themselves develop. Secondly, these qualities are chiefly connected with coming to see others and oneself as persons. Thirdly, this 'coming to see others as persons' can be broken down into (a) recognising that others have thoughts and feelings different from one's own; (b) extending this personal awareness to different categories of people; and (c) entering into personal relationships which incorporate this personal awareness. Fourthly, however, these qualities of 'being a person' refer to the increasing capacity to accept responsibility for what one does, an idea that often gets picked out by the concept of 'autonomy'.

3   Development into a Particular Sort of Person

A small-scale action research[2] into aspects of personal development of five- and six-year-olds examined the use of materials and teaching approaches which were aimed at developing the practice of sharing and co-operating. To share, rather than to be possessive, and to co-operate seemed to be important personal qualities to develop. Furthermore, their development seemed to depend upon how the children perceived social situations, as well as upon their acceptance of certain values. If this were the case, it seemed sensible for the research to examine ways and means of developing such qualities in early childhood.

It could be the case however that what seemed to the researcher to be central to personal development might not seem so to others, and this indeed became apparent. The prevailing values at some homes militated against sharing and co-operation where it was felt that an important stage in growing up was to assert oneself and to learn how to pursue one's own interests single-mindedly. Learning how to share, therefore, far from being regarded as essential to personal growth, was seen to be a particular value appreciated by (possibly) only a minority of people. Whether sharing and co-operation are to be valued depends upon the *sort* of person you want to produce, and upon the sort of future society you want to create. Furthermore, significant sex differences emerged even at a very young age. Boys were more assertive and competitive than girls, and such character traits were clearly encouraged by the values implicit in the social relationships and the attitudes of their homes.

It would seem important, therefore, to distinguish between those qualities which I argued for in the last section to be essential to development *as a person* (and which I shall enlarge upon in chapter 3) and those qualities and powers which, however important they seem to us, are not essential but depend upon particular values which some people hold but many certainly don't. The distinction may be rather rough and ready and, indeed, there is a large grey area where it would be disputed whether or not particular qualities and powers of the mind are central to being a person. But the distinction, for all its raggedness, does seem a valid one. There are qualities that are important because they are intimately connected with what we mean by someone being a person (and that we identify through analysing what we *mean* by 'personhood'), and there are qualities that we cherish because of specific values that we hold. Some schools attach considerable importance to punctuality, to obedience, to authority, to conformity in behaviour, to emphasising sex differences through uniform, games, or clubs. If made explicit, the reasons for such practices would reflect particular values in personal development, both the ends to be achieved and the best way of getting them. Such practices and values are not about developing *as persons* but about becoming the sort of person liked by that particular school.

Here I want to do no more than lay the foundations for later, more practical, consideration of the curriculum. Nearly every-thing one does in school is, either directly through the successful achievement of one's curriculum aims or indirectly through the unintended effects of what one is doing or the relationships one has with pupils, likely to have some effect upon the sort of person the pupil becomes. Personal and social values are implicit in, and conveyed through, the selection of books, the choice of certain activities rather than others, the attitude of teacher to teacher and to pupil, and the opinions expressed. None the less, in order to make sense of all this in curriculum terms, we need to make certain broad distinctions between the different kinds of values and knowledge which are relevant to development into this or that sort of person.

(a) **Intellectual virtues:** these are the dispositions such as 'con-cern for getting at the truth' or 'concern for matching conclusion to evidence' which are characteristic of persons engaged in intellectual enquiry. Some people have them, others don't – or rather some are more disposed than others to set about answering questions in ways that we morally approve of and that arise from the values inherent in any serious pursuit of the truth.

(b) **Moral virtues:** these are the dispositions such as modesty, kindness, patience, generosity, which govern the emotions. The kind person is he who *tends*, as Aristotle argued[3], to act kindly, that is, it becomes 'part of his nature' to treat other people with consideration and with a concern for their well-being. Different people do have different emotional dispositions and what actually should go into a list of moral virtues would not receive universal agreement. Tolerance is a virtue cherished by English liberals, but not by Iranian mullahs. Humility is a Christian virtue not shared by Homer's heroes. A great deal of early personal development consists in the encouragement of some dispositions at the expense of others. One can *become* kind and humble. What then are the dispositions that one wishes to encourage at school – and what are those that one seeks to discourage? What is a virtue for some (for example, modesty, humility, thrift) may for others be vices.

(c) **Character traits:** traditionally in philosophy a distinction has been made between moral and intellectual virtues on the

one hand and character traits on the other. The latter are
those qualities of the 'will' such as perseverance or courage.
Hitler may not have been very virtuous but he had – unfortunately – a strong character. Very often in the past certain
curriculum activities have been defended because they
strengthen the character or develop it in some way – learning
Latin irregular verbs or playing rugger on muddy pitches.
This may at times seem daft, but we do like pupils not only to
have the right sort of feelings but also to have the grit (or
graft) to see a job through once started. Are there qualities of
'will' which can be influenced (if not taught) through the life
and curriculum of schools?

(d)   **Social competencies:** in recent literature (see for example
FEU, 1980a) reference is made to 'social and life skills'. This
is an omnibus phrase that includes dispositions, sense of
responsibility, moral habits and worthwhile interests. This is
unfortunate because being virtuous (for example, being a
generous person) or acting responsibly or being thoughtful
(the qualities we normally associate with moral and personal
development) require more than acquiring skills, although
the moral life and personal qualities might require us to try to
learn such skills. A person might be considerate but lack the
social skills to act appropriately. On the other hand he might
have these skills, yet lack the readiness to employ them (or,
worse, have the skills and cynically employ them as though
he were considerate). How much importance therefore
should we attach to social competencies such as the ability to
sound pleasant in certain social situations, to command
respect, to deal with embarrassing situations with aplomb?
Social competencies could include the ability to deal with
certain kinds of social situations such as talking at cocktail
parties to unknown people about trivial matters. But it could
also include basic good manners, which although in one
sense conventional, in another sense embody and convey
certain kinds of attitudes and relationships. The boundary
between morality and etiquette is blurred in places, although
I feel that too much importance is attached even by schools to
the relatively trivial social competencies which fall well on
the etiquette side of the distinction.

(e)   **Practical knowledge:** quite apart from moral qualities and
social competencies we do often assess a person in terms of

practical abilities. We refer to someone as a practical person, meaning that in a wide range of practical tasks, such as repairing cars or DIY jobs in the home, he can generally solve problems and display intelligence. Or we refer to someone as a political person, meaning that he has quick practical grasp of political situations and can deal shrewdly with certain kinds of interpersonal problems. No doubt many aspects of our upbringing of children affect the sort of person someone becomes in this respect, and no doubt, too, a particular kind of school ethos, devaluing practical know-how and skills, will generate the sort of expectancies which will push children in a particular direction.

(f) **Theoretical knowledge:** in thinking out the sort of person one should become, one cannot ignore the understandings, concepts, beliefs, principles, insights that are afforded through theoretical study. Being a person, as opposed to a mere object, presupposes some developed form of consciousness. But that form of consciousness can be developed in different ways. A 'religious person' must have certain religious concepts and understandings. Deny him these and he would not be that sort of person. Or again, in the absence of political concepts (let us say, of a liberal democratic kind), then a person will have a different form of political consciousness that might well affect the sort of person he becomes – he sees things and thereby relates to people differently.

(g) **Personal values:** I spoke earlier about moral qualities and character traits. To develop these is connected, but not synonymous, with the acquiring of personal values. Two people could be equally gentle and considerate but disagree on the value of pacifism. Two people could be equally honest and yet disagree on the value of private property – to the extent that the same action might be seen as stealing by one and not by the other. In the documents referred to in chapter 1, it is argued that pupils should be helped to form their own stable set of personal values. These are not spelt out in any detail, possibly because positive suggestions would seem to encroach upon the essentially private world of the person. Indeed, one curriculum response to this view is a programme of 'values clarification', which I shall examine in chapter 4.

I have suggested therefore various aspects under which someone might be thought to be a 'person of a certain sort'. Personal
development, where it does not refer to development *as* a person,
would require some explicit account of the moral and intellectual
disposition, of the character traits, of the social competencies, of
the practical and theoretical knowledge, and of the personal values
that you want the pupil to acquire. This may at first seem
far-fetched, but should not do so upon reflection. A parent or
teacher is constantly promoting such virtuous dispositions as
considerateness, patience, or obedience; the teacher particularly
must be committed to intellectual virtues if she is seriously trying
to initiate her pupils into different forms of understanding. Certainly some parents attach considerable importance to specific
social competencies and send their children away to school to
ensure that they acquire them. Often, of course, such qualities,
traits, and knowledge remain only implicit in the exhortations, the
daily routine, and the relationships of most schools. But they are
still there, and curriculum development in this area must at least
begin with an attempt to make them explicit and to subject them to
analysis and criticism.

There would however be some point in doing so only if it were
thought that there was a rational way of sorting oneself through the
infinite range of possible dispositions, character traits, competencies, values and kinds of practical and theoretical knowledge
that one could promote – and if it were thought that such aims
when decided upon could be more easily reached through the
adoption of one teaching approach rather than another. Much of
this book will be concerned with seeing how far one can go in this
direction. But here it may be worth attending to the different sorts
of argument which those who wish to promote personal and social
development would need to justify it.

Firstly, assuming certain social and political values, the sort of
person one thinks should be developed would depend partly upon
the qualities thought necessary to maintain a particular kind of
society. Democracy requires a respect for the rule of law. The
maintenance of economic standards may require certain attitudes
towards the world of work as some British Prime Ministers have
argued.[4] And indeed that roughly was a main strand in Plato's
argument in *The Republic*. Different roles in society – those of
leader, guardian, and craftsman – required different qualities
and different training. Hence, one kind of argument for a programme of personal development relies upon some analysis of

those social and moral values which are central to our form of life.

Secondly, personal development incorporates some ideal of the moral person – the disposition and habits we would like to see him have. And this in turn requires some form of moral argument -- why the co-operative person is somehow preferable to the competitive one, or why the humble or retiring person is more to be valued than the self-assertive and proud one. I do not think, however, one can get very far in rational argument here. One can ultimately do little more than display one's ideal for others to see, and invite them to share that ideal.

Thirdly, personal development involves the acquisition of certain values, and these would need to be defended by moral argument, unless, of course, you believed that there was no such thing as valid moral argument, in which case you might simply revert to the techniques of values clarification in order to help the pupil 'to decide' upon his own set of values.

Fourthly, one might hold that the sort of person one should aim to produce depends upon the wishes of the consumer – the parents who provide the money, as well as the child, and who want, for whatever reason, a certain sort of product. Different schools are established to represent different personal and social ideals, and parents sometimes *choose* the one that most closely fits the image they want.

To summarise this briefly, schools that are interested in personal and social development need to be asked *what* sort of qualities they wish to see developed in young people. And it may be helpful to distinguish between intellectual qualities, moral virtues, character traits, social competencies, practical know-how, theoretical knowledge, personal values. Secondly, they need to discuss *why* these different qualities are worth promoting, and here they would need to consider the personal qualities required to maintain a particular form of social life, moral ideals, moral values, and the wishes of parents and others who, after all, are ultimately paying the bill.

The grey area, or indeed the shifting boundary, between those qualities considered central to someone's development as a person and those qualities which, though important, may not be considered central is reflected in the changing educational and social attitudes towards sex differentiation and sex related roles. Until very recently certain qualities were thought without question to be essentially feminine and thus to be fostered as part of a girl's development as a woman – essential to *her* personal development. Along with such unquestioned assumptions about feminine qualities went certain educational ideals, social aspirations, role expectations, ways of behaving and relating to other people – women as well as men. Once, however, these assumptions about 'the nature' of women and their place in society were questioned, the arguments about girls' and boys' education changed in kind. The onus of proof lay on the shoulders of those who wished to differentiate rather than the other way round. Furthermore, the argument for differentiation could no longer appeal to the distinctive nature of being a woman as though that could sustain all the differences in practice that we have been accustomed to. In the absence of any good argument for differentiated schooling then, schools should be trying to eradicate differences in provision and in opportunities. For the philosophical issues on this, one should read Radcliffe Richards (1980). On pages 123 and 139 I raise the issues in a more practical way. The main point here is that the *sort* of person one becomes will be related partly to how one sees one's sex to be a key element in what one can or should aspire to or in the images that influence one's own social relationships.

4   Respect for Persons

Finally in any general account of personal development we need to examine the place of 'respect for persons' as one element in that development. Is there something defective in my development if, despite having all the attributes which we have so far been talking about, I am totally lacking in respect for others as persons – or indeed for myself? Once again, at the common-sense level, teachers would regard the growth of respect for others and for oneself as central to personal development.

This is not, however, as easy to answer as it seems at first sight. There are many examples in history of people whom one could not deny to be fully persons – often 'much larger than life' persons – yet whose treatment of others left so much to be desired. Indeed, such disrespect seemed closely tied to their creativity and genius. Could we say, for example, that Beethoven was, in the light of his often quite thoughtless treatment of others and of his single-minded pursuit of creativity at the expense of others, thereby lacking in his personal development?

Perhaps too much can be made of this problem, but it raises rather graphically what we mean by respect for persons and how such respect for persons relates to other aspects of personal development.

Let us begin, therefore, by analysing the different levels at which one might be said to respect a person. First, there is the simple recognition of someone who has a mind of her own, has a distinctive point of view, and can provide an alternative perspective upon events. Very probably, when pressed, everyone might be said to respect everyone else as persons in this sense. But one needs to be wary here. It could be the case, as we have already noted, that such recognition may not, within particular cultures, be extended to certain groups of people – to people of different ethnic backgrounds or to children. And even where, when one is pressed, such recognition might be given, very often this may not happen in ordinary everyday relationships. I may, when pressed, be forced to admit that a child is a person in the sense of having a distinctive and reasonable point of view, but in practice I may demonstrate again and again my failure to see this – I simply disregard him or her as a person.

At this first level, therefore, my respect for someone as a person requires minimally the recognition in practice as well as in theory that he or she is capable of reasoning and reflecting, and thus has a point of view which, even if wrong, cannot be dismissed without being given serious attention.

Such a minimal notion of respect for persons contains no reference to caring about the feelings or the wants or the specific interests or the welfare of the other person – solely to his or her capacity for reasoning. It is therefore an important but none the less restricted sense of respect. Secondly, therefore, respect for persons refers to having an attitude towards other people in which their wants, feelings, and interests matter and not simply the points of view that they put across. To ignore such wants, feelings and interests is to ignore what is essentially individual and particular about them as persons. It is to say that their intentions and aspirations are of no account in whatever plans I have. They are to be discounted, as it were, even in my more altruistic attempts to improve general welfare and happiness. Respect for persons, therefore, at the second level, requires the development of this caring for other people in the sense that one recognises that their intentions, and feelings, and aspirations matter and should be taken into account. Furthermore, the deepening of this respect would lie in the enhancement of the recognition of how others do in fact feel and of what they aspire to. Being able to feel things from another's point of view is part of respecting him or her as someone who has distinctive feelings.

At no time, however, should respecting persons be confused with liking, let alone loving, them. Good *personal* relationships do not require having an affection for the person I am relating to. Indeed, affectionate personal relationships could get in the way of personal respect in so far as sometimes these might be of a selfish nature, blinding one to the real interests and welfare of the other, or being pursued irrespective of those interests. Or they might get in the way of developing respectful relationships with others in the group. Very often respect requires keeping one's distance a little. Certainly it is wrong to confuse it with affection.

These are, if correct, important distinctions to make. Too often teachers seek, out of a mistaken understanding of respect for persons, deeper personal involvement with pupils than is either necessary or desirable. Or, again, teachers can sometimes feel that the aversion they have for a particular person is indicative of a lack of respect. One must, so the reaction might be, try harder to like the pupil. But this is mistaken. I can dislike someone, but respect him just the same. I can see beneath the personality to the person, and recognise that for what it is, and act towards him or her accordingly.

On the other hand, there are appropriate feelings connected with having respect for another person. To recognise someone as a person is not a purely cognitive act. There is an appropriate feeling or tendency towards that person. And this indeed can be fostered by getting people to put themselves in the other's place, to seek, to feel, and to see as the other feels and sees, and to attend to the uniqueness of the other's position. To recognise and to attend to others as persons is to see them from a distinctive point of view in a feeling sort of way. They matter, and that is recognised not in a purely disinterested and cerebral manner but with feeling and with the tendency to do something about it. And all that is distinct from liking them.

Respect for persons therefore is, as Downie and Telfer (1969, page 16) point out, both an attitude and a principle. It is an attitude in the sense that one has, in recognising the other as a person, an active sympathy with how the other sees and feels about things and a detestation of the purely instrumental use or manipulation of someone else. It is a principle in that one prescribes to oneself that one should try to understand the other's point of view and how the other feels about matters. Furthermore by following the principle of respecting others, by dutifully trying to adopt an active caring for others, one might thereby develop the appropriate attitude.

5 Conclusion and Questions

Such an account of being a person does furnish us with a set of criteria, and thus of questions, with which to approach practice. For example, it would not show respect for a person if one always excused any wrong doing by referring to such circumstances as adverse upbringing, unhealthy environment, physical incapacity, since this would be to say that he was entirely the victim of external forces – that he had no control over or responsibility for what he did. To deny the distinction between naughtiness and mental ill health (reflected in the desire by some to turn all prisons into hospitals) is to disvalue people as persons.[5] Again, to teach without coming to grips with how the learner understands things, or to provide a particular course of studies without relating it to the students' consuming interests, would be to impose a system of ideas or a set of values that disrespect the learner as a person. It is as though he is an object to be changed or altered for other purposes – those of the teacher or of the community represented by the teacher. He is not respected as a person – as someone with a conscious view of things and of what is of value. Yet again, one might be critical of certain methods of teaching in that they do not allow for the critical questioning by the learner. In that a child has a mind he is, even at a very young age, a source of criticism of the ideas put forward by the teacher or parent. To muzzle such criticism or not to allow scope for it, especially in those matters that affect the learner's interests, would be to neglect an essential feature of him *as a person*.

We might therefore ask of the curriculum and of the other experiences pupils are receiving in schools: does the curriculum, for example,

(i)   respect pupils as people who can think, that is, have their own ideas and points of view, capable of contributing to the various explorations, enquiries, or activities that children and adults engage in?

(ii)   assist pupils to see others as persons whatever their colour, creed or appearance?

(iii) enable pupils to see themselves as persons, able not only to think and to reflect and to develop a point of view, but also to accept responsibility for their own behaviour and future?

(iv) foster that attitude of respect for oneself and others as persons, that is, as people that have legitimate points of view and that can and should be held responsible for what is done?

Schools that are keen to develop personal and social education in their curriculum should start by asking these questions about the impact of the curriculum as a whole upon the pupils. To put yet another subject on the timetable can so easily be a distraction from the real issues.

NOTES

1 For a detailed analysis of the concept of education and of the conceptual connections between it and a worthwhile form of life and specifically human values, one should read Peters (1966) *Ethics and Education*, chapters 1, 2 and 5, and the subsequent development of these ideas in his essay 'Education and the educated man' (see Peters, 1970, republished in Peters, 1977).

2 The research on developing social awareness in young children was conducted by Olwen Goodall under the direction of Dr David Evans at the Centre for the Study of Personal, Social, and Moral Education at the University of Exeter School of Education. It was funded for four years by the St Luke's Trust. It developed out of close co-operation with teachers in local schools, and has produced valuable curriculum materials and suggestions for classroom practice which are the basis of further work. (See Goodall *et al.*, 1983.)

3 See Aristotle's Nichomachaean *Ethics*, Penguin edition, 1953, especially Book 2. One can detect in the history of ethics two very different traditions. One, rooted in Aristotle, identifies the good person with the one who has certain dispositions or qualities – who 'naturally' does what is right. The other, more closely associated with the philosopher Kant, identifies the good person with the one who has 'a good will', that is the one who acts out of a sense of duty, irrespective of what his or her dispositions are. These distinctions are very important in our moral appraisal of people, and indeed in considering the moral upbringing of children, as I hope this book will illustrate.

4 James Callaghan, when Prime Minister, gave a speech at Ruskin

College, Oxford, in October 1976, in which he criticised the failure of the educational service for not relating the curriculum closely enough to the needs of the world of work. This has become a regular theme in subsequent DES and HMI publications, and indeed it lies behind a lot of the initiative of the MSC.

5 The philosopher Kant stressed 'good will' as the most important moral quality of a person – the capacity to act according to one's sense of duty rather than according to whatever feelings or tendencies happened to influence one. To understand this, one needs to distinguish between *causal* explanations of what happened ('I was *made* to jump' or 'I could not help blinking') and explanations in terms of the reason and self-determination of the agent ('I jumped to avoid the car' or 'I winked in order to show I did not mean what I said'). The danger of some social reformers is that, in neglecting this distinction, everything that a person does is explained in terms of causes. Therefore the agent is no longer held responsible for what he or she does – and thus in need of treatment rather than punishment. Those who wish to pursue this in depth should read Kant's 1785 work on ethics, but the issue is raised, in the context of medicine and social work, throughout Downie and Telfer's recent (1980) book *Caring and Curing*.

3 Personal Development: A Theoretical Perspective

1 Development

Parents and teachers are interested not simply in how children behave and think now but in the relation of what happens now to how the children will behave and think in the future. Put crudely, their interest lies in development. That is, they want to know what they need to do at an early age in order to ensure that the children will turn out 'good' people, 'integrated personalities', behaving in a 'correct and acceptable' manner, with the ability to think 'sensibly' and to make 'wise' judgments. (Each person will of course have his own view about what is good, integrated, correct, sensible and wise, but this in no way affects the general point about development.) What connections are there between the thinking and behaving of a five-year-old and her thinking and behaving five, ten or fifteen years later? What can be said about the *development* from one period to another?

We have already in chapter 2 anticipated one kind of answer to these questions, namely, that changes which take place in a person 'grow out of' earlier stages systematically and according to certain general principles. Later stages of development are seen as an improvement upon earlier ones whilst at the same time presupposing them. Phrases like 'realising his or her potential' capture the flavour of it. It is as though the fully developed person is already there embryonically in the young child, just as the oak tree is potentially there in the acorn; it simply needs to be properly fed and nurtured.

There are dangers in this way of thinking. An exaggerated stress upon development underplays the importance of learning – the acquisition of concepts, habits, skills, beliefs, qualities of character, which arise, not from the development of some inner potential, but from instruction, initiation, and 'external' influences of a social kind. We cannot let children simply grow into morally mature adults in this very complex world. There is a great deal they need to be taught. None the less, the *capacity* to recognise others as persons, and to see things from their point of view, to examine moral issues in the light of general principles, or to accept responsibility for one's actions, does itself seem to develop. And it is to making sense of this notion of development that we turn in this chapter. If correct, such a theoretical perspective has considerable implications for personal and social education.

The features of development in the sense we are talking about are:

(i)   it can be broken up into *distinct stages*;
(ii)   each stage demonstrates a *qualitatively different mode of functioning*;
(iii) each stage is a *structural transformation of a previous stage* – it re-structures in a more adequate way the previous mode of operating;
(iv)   the *stage sequence is irreversible*, the earlier stages necessarily preceding the later ones;
(v)   the process of development can stop at any stage (thus we talk of stunted growth).

What are transformed stage by stage in personal development are those characteristics of 'personhood' that I picked out in chapter 2, namely the ways in which one thinks, feels, and behaves in a meaningful and responsible way. It is the capacity to see things, to reflect upon them, to form judgments, to relate to others, and to behave accordingly which is transformed in a qualitative way. Of course, different children will learn different ideas, habits, beliefs, and skills, but the way in which they learn will be 'structured' according to the stage of development they are at. Whatever the differences in *content* of what children learn, there will be similarities in the *formal organisation* of this content. These concepts of 'structure' and 'transformation of structure' and the distinction between 'form' and 'content' are vital for understanding development in the sense we shall be considering, and I shall clarify them as we proceed.

2 Rule-following and Intentionality

In *The Moral Judgment of the Child*, Piaget (1932) sets himself two main tasks. First, he wants to investigate what is meant by respect for rules from the child's point of view. Secondly, he seeks to analyse those notions, especially that of 'justice', which seem central to the way in which people relate to one another. Why, in a book of this title, should Piaget have been so concerned with 'respect for rules'? He does at the very beginning explain that 'all morality consists in a system of rules and the essence of all morality is to be sought in the respect which the individual acquires for these rules'.

There is, I believe, a mistaken emphasis here which, as I shall show later, can lead to a rather unbalanced view of both personal and moral development. None the less, it is quite clearly true that 'morals' are very largely concerned with what one ought or ought not to do, and thus with rules of behaviour. Hence, the attitude towards rules and the ability to act consistently in accordance with them are without doubt central to moral, and thus to personal, development.

Piaget argues that as the child grows older there is a gradual transformation of the way he or she applies rules and of his or her consciousness of rules. It is this transformation in what, to Piaget, is the central feature of moral behaviour which characterises the moral development of the child.

Before we attend to this in some detail, two important points should be noted which are highlighted by Piaget. First, he distinguishes the application of rules from the consciousness of what one is thus doing in practice. One can know *how* to do something (and exercise that knowledge) without necessarily knowing *that* (in any conscious sense) one is doing it. And, indeed, for Piaget the later stages of cognitive development are the conscious realisation of what is already implicit in one's behaviour.

Secondly, the transformation both in the practice and in the consciousness of rules refers, not to changed rule-following habits or to the acquisition of new rules, but to a structural change through which rules are understood in a very different manner. The idea of structural change is of central importance to the rather strong sense of development that we are here considering. A given structure has certain parts or elements which are related to each other in terms of some defined order. It is this relationship between parts which provides the unity of the thing in question, and the parts or elements can change without the structure changing. 'Structure' therefore is to be understood in contrast with 'content'. Content refers to the parts or elements of a person's mental life – the particular beliefs or habits or concepts that he or she has. Structure refers to the way in which these are held and related to each other. Two people may hold different beliefs but hold them in a significantly similar way – the 'logic' of their thinking has a lot in common. Likewise two people may hold what on the surface look like the same belief but what upon further investigation are significantly different ways of holding these beliefs. Central to understanding Piaget and the social psychologists we shall be examining in this chapter is to see that it is the way in which thought is organised, rather than the content of that thought, which is gradually being changed and that the change consists of a transformation of previous ways of thinking to something 'more adequate'. In pursuing his investigations, Piaget was looking for the 'inner logic' – the underlying structure – of the reasoning of children rather than the specific thoughts they had.

What then is this changing structure that characterises a child's practice or application of rules? When only a baby, the child will engage in behaviour that could not be described as rule-governed – although he will come to see regularities in events and thus will have expectations accordingly. Soon, however, the child will learn that there are rules – after all very quickly he has to learn certain rules about regular meals, washing, not hitting other children, and so on. The child will learn, too, rules of playing games. But the resulting rule-following exists side by side with little sense of co-operation – of seeing these rules as part of a social form of life through which co-operation between individuals is regulated. The ability to see things in this social perspective is lacking, and it is this which Piaget referred to as the state of ego-centrism. The major transformation therefore that affects the very nature of rule-following behaviour at every level lies in this gradual shift to what is called 'incipient co-operation' where a social perspective becomes possible. This involves working within what is seen to be a framework of common rules and this is reflected in the pleasure that youngsters find in the playing of games – in competing within a shared system of rules. Finally, youngsters reach the stage in which they can think through these rules systematically – the codification of rules.

Alongside this changing practice of rules is a developing consciousness of what one is doing. At the very beginning, rules are not coercive; they are not received as obligations. Soon, however, some rules are seen to have this obligatory character. Rules arise from powerful figures such as mother and father and are not to be tampered with. The respect that the child has for the authors of these rules (after all they are powerful figures who do command respect through their insistence upon a multitude of rules such as those of cleaning teeth before bed, saying 'please' when one asks for anything, kissing one's parents before going to sleep) is transferred to the rules themselves. They are somehow 'sacred', part of the fabric of the universe. The attitude towards the rules is related to what Piaget refers to as the 'unilateral respect' the child has for the authors of the rules. One aspect of this respect for rules is the relative insignificance attached by the child to the intentions or to the point of view of the person who breaks the rule. For example, the young child will probably judge more harshly the person who breaks several glasses unintentionally than the person who breaks one glass intentionally. But even when much older a youngster (or grown-up) may insist that a rule is a rule and not to be broken under any circumstances. There is often a lack of sympathy for mitigating circumstances.

Finally, the growing child will come to see rules essentially as regulations of social activity that are to be respected, not as something sacred or unchangeable, but as rationally defensible parts of social relationships which require mutual recognition and agreement amongst those whom they concern. The intentions of those who break the rules are crucial to the ascription of responsibility. There is an awareness of the other's point of view as something relevant to adaptation of rules which ultimately are there to serve mutually agreed social purposes.

It should be remembered that these very important changes in the structure of rule governed activity and of the way in which the child is conscious of it are untidy. Piaget does not speak of clear cut stages. Rather is it the case that the continuity in change makes 'arbitrary any attempt to cut mental reality up into stages' (page 78). It is really a matter of proportion, for there is an element of the adult form of thought (recognising intentionality, seeing some rules as changeable) in even the very young child, and there remains an element of the child's form of thought in the grown-up. For example, in strictly conformist societies there will be a greater degree of the 'unilateral respect' for authority with a consequent experience of rules as unquestionable and superimposed from outside. The promotion of moral growth on this view would lie, not in a simple shift from one mode of consciousness to another, but in the gradual extension of mutual or rational respect, and of the recognition of intentionality in ascribing responsibility, to different areas of social life and of personal relations.

Put simply, the basic structural change with regard to rules (and thus to morality in so far as it is concerned with rule-governed activity) lies in a shift from what Piaget calls *heteronomy*, where rules are given by external authorities ('morality of constraint') and where the rules tend to be 'objective' and unchangeable ('moral realism'), to autonomy, where rules are mutually agreed and internalised ('morality of co-operation') and thus can be adapted to changing situations. Typical of heteronomy, but not of autonomy, is the little regard paid to the intentionality and perspectives of the other person in ascribing responsibility. It should be remembered however that such a simple way of putting it does not do justice to the different degrees to which a person may see rules to be essentially external and unchangeable, or authority to be respected reverentially, or the other's subjective state of mind (intentions, mental state) to be taken into account in the passing of judgment. It is essentially a matter of proportion, and different circumstances will doubtless provoke different degrees in this structural shift.

Two further comments need to be made. First, Piaget is providing an account of development in the strong sense that I described, in that (i) the change is directed towards a more improved state of both behaving and understanding, and (ii) each stage of the change presupposes an earlier stage which is then transformed or qualitatively altered. The 'improvement' lies in a more accurate as well as an adequate appreciation of the nature of rules – adequate in the sense that the subsequent practice and consciousness of rules enables a form of social life more adaptable to changing social circumstances.

Secondly, at the centre of this shift from heteronomy to autonomy is the relationship with authority and the degree of co-operative behaviour which is permitted or encouraged, for the shift from morality of constraint to the morality of co-operation arises part and parcel with the requirements of collaborative social life. This quite clearly is inhibited by a strong insistence upon unilateral respect. Essential therefore to the promotion of development as it is here described will be the gradual encouragement of mutual or rational respect for rules at the expense of unilateral respect, the consequent diminishing of authority, and the creation of more co-operative forms of social life. Failure of educational institutions to do this could have two different sorts of consequence. Firstly, the child might remain in a highly dependent state of mind, relying upon others to sort out his or her moral and personal questions, unable to bend a little to appreciate the other's point of view, anxious about deviations from the norms that he or she has acquired, and unable to cope with social circumstances not anticipated by the old rules. Secondly, however, the pupil who has, through the informal education of peers or of home, already progressed some way beyond the stage of moral realism and the morality of constraint, will find irksome the assumption of the school that still insists upon such a morality, and insists upon that unilateral respect for authority which the pupil is quickly growing out of. Such a child might respond sullenly, or might choose to 'play the game' though without any respect for its authors, or might instead find the constraints too great to withstand and break out in open rebellion. There is no doubt in my mind that any school that is serious about the personal development of its young people must address itself first to the nature and exercise of authority within that school.

At the very young or infant level, we are witnessing of course the slow development of the ability to apply rules within an essentially social framework and to see that others have distinctive points of view which need to be taken into account. Collaborative play only slowly supersedes the parallel play of an earlier stage, and requires encouragement. The submission to rules in a consistent manner is an ability and a disposition acquired painfully and with difficulty as any adult knows who has played board games with very young children. But it is essential for personal development.

3   Moral Judgment and a Sense of Justice

The work of Piaget inspired many to think of personal development, not in the weak sense of acquiring whatever ways of behaving and of thinking were appropriate to some specific goal, but in the strong sense of a gradual transformation of the structure of mental life which made how we think, and how we behave, *qualitatively* different. The lesson, crudely speaking, that schools might draw from this is that they should concentrate not so much upon acquiring moral or personal knowledge or skills or concepts, but upon the improvement of the *quality* of what children are already doing, or how they are already thinking, even at a very young age. That at any rate is the idea behind the teachers' education workshops arising out of the work of Lawrence Kohlberg.

Kohlberg and his colleagues have for thirty years been investigating the structure of young people's thinking about moral issues. Like Piaget, they did this through probing the reasons that children gave in answer to certain moral dilemmas. Furthermore, much of the investigation was a longitudinal study[1] so that one could see the nature of the change in the sort of reasons they gave. The conclusion of the investigation is that people think about moral issues in six qualitatively different stages, or at three different levels (the preconventional level of moral reasoning, the conventional level, and the post-conventional level) with two stages at each level. Each stage is characterised by a determinate *structure* or organisation of thinking (irrespective of its particular *content*) and this organisation changes, in suitable circumstances, to a better, more adequate organisation which transforms the previous structure. Kohlberg is concerned with *moral* cognitive development – that is, the gradual improvement of the quality or structure of our thinking about moral matters – but one can see how it complements Piaget's work on rule-following and intentionality, as well as of course Piaget's better known work on intellectual development.

Put very briefly, Kohlberg's map of cognitive moral development suggests the following 'orientation' in people's moral reasoning:

Level 1:   Pre-conventional

The overriding reason for doing what is right (or avoiding what is wrong) lies in the pursuit of self-interest rather than in any 'objective' grounds – the fear of punishment, the pursuit of reward, the obtaining of pleasure.

Stage 1:   Heteronomous morality
The physical consequences of what one does determine whether it is good or bad – it receives punishment or it warrants reward; it is enjoined by a powerful authority.

Stage 2:   Instrumentalism
That is good or bad which serves one's own interests, whilst at the same time one recognises the need to accommodate those of others

('I'll scratch your back if you'll scratch mine' kind of reasoning). Children are very concerned about fairness, but usually when their interests (not Dad's) are at issue and when they are concerned that what they do is in return for benefits received.

Level 2:   Conventional

Actions are right or values are to be held not because they serve one's own interest (although they might do that as well) but because they are 'objectively' good – the conventional norms of the wider social group whether family, peers, or society as a whole. The maintenance of this social order is very important.

Stage 3:   Interpersonal relationship and conformity
What is approved (or gains approval) from significant others is what is right – the conventions of one's milieu concerning one's role as son, daughter, pupil. There is considerable emphasis upon trust and loyalty.

Stage 4:   Social system maintenance
The importance of social conventions extends to society as a whole, and these conventions are seen to be justified in terms of the maintenance of society, for keeping the law is terribly important, as is respecting authority and doing one's social duty.

Level 3:   Post-conventional

At this level people look beyond conventional morality to more universal principles from which they can be critical of what is received wisdom.

Stage 5:   Social contract and individual rights
People can contrast what they see to be an individual's rights with the received norms of a society (which could, for instance, be racialist in its conventions). They look beyond conventional definitions of right and wrong to more general values of human welfare. Conventional laws are upheld as much as possible because the maintenance of contracts can generally (but not on all occasions) be justified in terms of human welfare.

Stage 6:   Universal ethical principles
People go back to ultimate principles which, after due thought, they believe they can universalise – for example, respect for people as persons irrespective of idiosyncracies or beliefs or race, equal liberty and justice for all – and which it is thought any human being would agree to if he or she viewed things quite impartially

('from behind a veil of ignorance'[2] as far as his or her interests are concerned).

Kohlberg argues that these different orientations characterise all moral thinking, but that progression from earlier stages to later ones can be halted at any point. Only a minority of people, for example, get beyond Stage 4 and many get stuck much earlier. What is not possible is for any stage to be omitted in the transition. The cause of the change from a lower to a higher stage is the experienced inadequacy of the lower stage of reasoning. It simply fails to resolve the kind of problems one is confronted with. One needs to resort, first, to more 'objective' values to sort out differences between people and, secondly, to a more universal principle when conventional morality does not provide a satisfactory answer to differences between cultures.

The method adopted by Kohlberg for his enquiry was that of asking young people of different ages what they thought was the answer to a particular moral dilemma. The dilemma lay in the necessary choice between two values – property or life, loyalty to friends or telling the truth, and so on. But the actual conclusion reached was not so important as the *kind* of reasons given and, with the help of considerable probing, it could be shown that the reasons would be one of six kinds set out above. One well-known dilemma (though there are several of them) was about Heinz who, having discovered that the only possible way of saving a young woman neighbour's life was to steal a new drug from its inventor, had the following choice to make: should he steal the drug or let the young neighbour die? The story does of course receive a little more embroidery. None the less, it is interesting to see the different responses one gets at different ages to such a dilemma. More interesting however are the differences in the reasons given. By scoring the reasons, Kohlberg and his followers claim that they are able to identify the stage of moral reasoning which that child (or indeed adult) is at. (See Colby *et al.* (1983a), Colby *et al.* (1983b), and Kohlberg (1983), chapters 8 and 11, for the details of scoring.)

For example, in work that I was engaged in, using Kohlberg's example (above), one boy aged 11 argued, in supporting his claim that Heinz should not steal the drug, that, if he did, he might get caught and put into prison. Another, the same age, argued that it all depended upon what the young neighbour had ever done for him. Yet a third objected that stealing is wrong and simply should not be engaged in whatever the consequences. These are examples, respectively, of the first three stages of moral reasoning. Of course, it is not quite as simple as that. Many young people would be at a transitional stage, and the quality of their reasoning might partly depend upon the topic being reasoned about. But the probing questions detailed in the *Scoring Manual* were seeking competence rather than performance and, if pursued by a trained scorer, would be able to get beneath such apparent variations and to discover the deeper level of reasoning that a child is capable of.

The use of dilemmas to identify the stage of moral reasoning is essentially a research tool, and one that needs to be used carefully by trained interviewers if one is to feel confident in the conclusions drawn. But the ability to reason about and to resolve moral dilemmas, and the quality of that reasoning, are quite clearly important aspects of personal development. The curriculum development work of Fenton and others shows that properly led moral discussions could bring about considerable improvements in young people's ability to reason about moral issues (see Colby *et al.*, 1977). Rarely, however, will young people get beyond Stage 4 before the age of sixteen, or indeed before eighteen. And in very traditional societies where there may be considerable consensus on what is right and wrong, and where there is little exposure to alternative viewpoints, Kohlberg and his colleagues discovered little or no evidence of reasoning at the post-conventional level. This indeed seems prima facie to be plausible, for what 'forces' one to think in a post-conventional way is precisely the failure of the appeal to convention where one is exposed to societies or other social groups which, though quite clearly having moral codes, do not accept the same criteria of what is good or bad. In resolving the difference, one is forced into considering more universal principles of justice and of respect for persons.

There are two ways in which a person's ability to reason about moral issues might be limited. The first is the person's intellectual ability; if a person finds 'formal operations', as referred to by Piaget, very difficult (namely, the ability to think in fairly abstract and hypothetical terms), then he is not going to be able to think in terms of the underlying principles of justice, abstracted from the 'concrete' morality of one's particular social group. Secondly, however much developed is one's formal ability to reason (one might be a quite brilliant mathematician), one might still lack the ability to see things from the other's point of view – to 'step into the other's shoes' – and this is surely a pre-condition of thinking about issues impartially rather than from one's own self-interest.

This brings us back, of course, to what we were saying, in connection with Piaget, about the gradual change from 'egocentrism', in which the only perspective that one can appreciate is one's own (one simply doesn't see that others might see things differently), to altruism where one can appreciate that others may have a different point of view and different feelings. This changing ability might be expressed as a developing capacity for 'role-taking', and it is the stage by stage development of this ability which was charted by Kohlberg's colleague Robert Selman.

Selman (1976) identifies successive stages in the development of a person's ability to appreciate the perspective of another: the ability of the child (i) to realise his perspective is different from that of others; (ii) to co-ordinate his perspective with that of others which he sees to be different; and (iii) to improve upon his differentiation yet co-ordination of perspectives. In attempting to chart this progressive development, Selman, like Kohlberg, uses the clinical interview technique to get at the social perspective of children who are trying to resolve a dilemma (for example, that of Heinz already referred to). Selman lists the following stages of 'role-taking':

Stage 0:

The child simply doesn't see things from the other's point of view.

Stage 1:   Social-informational role-taking

The child understands that others may have a different point of view (that others have intentions, act with purpose and for reasons), but these differences arise simply because each has different information. If only the others had the same information as the subject, he would *feel* about things in the same way.

Stage 2:   Self-reflective role-taking

The child realises that another person may feel differently about a situation, even when there is no disagreement on facts. Furthermore he can see that the other may have conflicts of feeling and of values. Again, the child becomes able to see how others might see him and, in interpreting his behaviour, react in a particular way to him.

Stage 3:   Mutual role-taking

The youngster can now look at interpersonal situations more impartially – as a spectator might look at and judge things without taking part. Each person in the relationship can simultaneously see the other's point of view, and come to terms with it in speaking and acting.

Stage 4:   Social and conventional system role-taking

This mutuality of understanding of different view points is extended to a much wider social group – to the 'generalised other' – and results in an appreciation of law and moral rules based on agreed group perspective. One sees other persons as having viewpoints that have resulted from a complex internalisation of norms, rules, feelings and beliefs.

The significance of Selman's work does of course go much further than in relation to a person's ability to reason about moral issues. Persons act, and therefore their development takes place, in social or interpersonal contexts. The quality of those interpersonal relations depends upon the way in which they are able to see things from another's point of view and to co-ordinate these different points of view in seeing things 'as a whole'. One's ability in this respect will affect (i) general social problem-solving (how to play games with other children or indeed how to work as a team in an integrated curriculum); (ii) the ability to persuade other people of one's own point of view; (iii) the appreciation of how others think and feel about situations. It is difficult to see how one can take personal development seriously without the promotion of the ability to take on the role and perspectives of others. And, particularly, it can be argued that a person's moral reasoning will be severely limited without the ability to adopt a wider social perspective. Certainly, they would not reach Stage 4 on Kohlberg's moral reasoning scales.

There are inevitably problems in these accounts which critics have been prompt to point out. Four, in particular, we should be aware of. First, there is the philosophical criticism that nothing follows from the fact that one stage necessarily succeeds another to that stage being superior to another. One cannot derive an 'ought' from an 'is', as philosophers have been fond of telling us. It is wrong, in other words, to assume that the autonomous person, acting from internalised principles that he is prepared to apply impartially to all irrespective of personal advantage, is necessarily morally superior to the person who takes on board the conventional morality of his society or church or clan, and sticks to it through thick and thin. Morality has a content, and a life of unquestioning honesty, kindness, and sobriety might be regarded as superior to the reflective and principled life where the principles permit stealing, hostile behaviour, and self-indulgence.

A second and connected philosophical objection is that Kohlberg's idea of moral improvement is a narrow one, dealing with only one (albeit an important) aspect of moral development. There is much more to moral growth than the developing ability to reason in a principled manner about what one ought to do when faced by a dilemma. Indeed, facing dilemmas is not the central feature of a moral life. More often than not we respond to situations fairly spontaneously and habitually, depending upon the dispositions that we have. Moral education is as much about the right kind of feelings or emotions as it is about acting from principles.

Thirdly, therefore, it is said that there is too much stress upon the purely cognitive aspect of morality – the moral judgment – without any clear indication of how this connects with moral action. After all it is what youngsters do rather than what they think that worries the public at large.

Finally, the stress upon development in the strong sense is seen by some as a devaluation of learning – where learning means the acquisition of certain ways of thinking, through teaching or through following examples or through 'picking up' the values that prevail within society at large.

I do not think that these objections, though they contain some truth, invalidate the general drift of the developmental argument. The criticism and the counter arguments are too complex to deal with in detail here, and indeed the next chapter will address itself to the wider issues of moral development, the place of emotions and feelings and the connection between thinking and doing. But the idea of development as the gradual transformation of the quality of a person's thinking, where this quality can be characterised at different stages in terms of certain dominant principles of reasoning or of certain conceptual structures or of certain motivating reasons, seems well substantiated and of considerable importance for programmes of personal development. There is, however, one social psychologist who brings this developmental tradition more directly to bear upon the development of a person in a more comprehensive sense and whose work has had some impact upon curriculum development in the USA. To her we now turn.

4 Ego Development

This rather pretentious title draws attention to the fact that the developing person is more than a collection of specific lines of development – of intellect, of the ability to see others' points of view, of moral reasoning, and so on. The 'self' which is the subject of all these, does itself seem to be an object in need of development. We do talk about someone disintegrating as a person, being immature, irresolute, weak-willed, and so on and there is a need for growth, for strengthening, for finding or for discovering oneself. Furthermore, in the absence of this development, there may be a lack of self-respect or self-esteem. People have a poor view of themselves, losing self-confidence, and acting in relation to others accordingly. For example, programmes for the young unemployed, whose school lives have often meant nothing but failure, need to help them to survive psychologically as well as economically. An increasingly common phrase used of a child is that he or she has a poor self-concept.

This, however, is a hard notion to grasp. It is rarely clear upon analysis what is meant by 'self-concept'. And the reason for this is that the self, if an object at all, is one of a rather peculiar sort, difficult to pick out and to examine. To some extent we have already introduced the notion in analysing the concept of person in the last chapter. A person is more than a physical thing – and a poor view of oneself as a person therefore involves more than a poor image of one's physical prowess. Furthermore one is more than a set of thoughts, a bundle of perceptions, a set of feelings. One is the *author* in some way of these – that which unites all these as the thoughts and feelings and aspirations of a single being. One cannot really observe the 'self' directly, as one might be said to observe tables, chairs, or other human beings. The 'self' is that which one presupposes as the necessary condition for all these things occurring.

I make no apology for speaking so obscurely. I have spent ages, sober and merry, trying to observe my 'self' – but can only get at aspects of it. And yet I cannot get away from there being some essential unity to all these aspects which itself can be either strengthened and integrated or weakened and dissipated.

This essential unity of being is reflected in such notions as 'authentic', 'being true to oneself', 'characteristic behaviour', 'in control of one's life' or 'responsible for one's actions'. Furthermore, we do even at the everyday level assume that it is something to be achieved. Young people are said not to be sure of their identity – it is something still to be discovered or created; education is sometimes said to be a process of self-realisation, an inner core of being which requires 'bringing out'; children need to gain control of those wayward feelings which push them hither and thither in often unpredictable ways. As Peters said, 'Where id was, there ego shall be'.

Faced, however, with such tantalising obscurity, how can one talk about the development of this self – rather than the development of *aspects* of it – intellect, reason, perception? Certainly it would be a development of a very complex fabric of how one relates to other people, of how one controls impulses, of disposition and character traits, of conscious preoccupations, of cognitive capacities and styles. Can any sense of unity or integration be discerned in all these which, in some recognisable sense, can be said to develop? Cognitive development itself, though necessary for the development of oneself as a person, is not sufficient. It might explain the ability to know but not to relate oneself to others as persons. Or, again, moral cognitive development, as explained by Kohlberg and his associates, might explain the ability to reason about values, but it says little about the attachment to values.

Often in trying to get to grips with this 'self' and its development, we are presented with theoretical models and metaphors – from psychoanalysis, from social psychology, from role play and drama. For example, there is the 'reflected' or 'looking glass' self in which one sees that the origin of 'self' lies in the social relationships one finds oneself in and in the internalisation of an ideal self which in turn is a reflection of what is discovered in those relationships. Or, similarly, there is Mead's argument that social behaviour is antecedent to the development of consciousness and that consciousness arises when we learn to represent ourselves to ourselves and to others. There is a growing awareness of self and a developing identity of one's own uniqueness in the presentation of oneself to others, and thus to oneself as others might see one. Or, again, we cannot ignore the debt we owe to the psychoanalysts' account of how we learn to cope with instinctive drives or certain kinds of feeling and attachments, and acquire mastery over these.

All this is beyond the scope of this book or indeed my capacity to relate together these different theoretical perspectives. The value of any theoretical perspective however is that it reminds us of key elements in the situation which otherwise, even at the relatively common-sense and practical everyday context in which teachers are working, we are in danger of ignoring. Personal development *is* inseparably bound to the social relationships through which that development takes place – the attachments one makes, the values one comes to hold, the ideals upon which one comes to model one's own strivings or against which one measures one's own failings. Early childhood *is* characterised by strong and wayward feelings (witness those awful tantrums, especially in the years of infancy, but also, for many, well into adolescence) which need to be mastered if one is to relate to other people in an acceptable manner or indeed simply to survive. Furthermore, the charting of different stages of intellectual development or of moral reasoning, though quite clearly of crucial importance, have only a limited significance in this growth of self-consciousness, of a sense of identity, of self-control, and of personal ideals. Therefore, without going into too much theoretical detail, teachers do need to know if any general pattern of personal development can be given which is wider than that of intellectual or moral reasoning. The work of Jane Loevinger attempts to do this. Loevinger (1976) talks of the 'ego' rather than the 'self', and the ego might be characterised as a rather complex 'fabric' of character traits, ways of interrelating with other people, conscious pre-occupations, capacities for controlling impulses, and modes of thinking about different issues. Those who feel disappointed at such a mixture of characteristics, rather than the identification of a 'thing' we call 'ego', must, I am afraid, be satisfied with the metaphor 'fabric' (in which different 'strands' of development intertwine), but that is the nature of the problem. The significant points, however, that Loevinger is making are that all these different features need to be taken into account in our characterisation of the 'self', that they interrelate, and that, as a complex 'fabric', it can be said to develop in a significant and meaningful way. Let me set out the general line of ego development as Loevinger sees it.

Stage 1:   Pre-social

The baby is very much guided by reflexes and moulded by the environment. He or she comes to appreciate there is a world separate from him/herself.

Stage 2:   Impulsive

The baby, although with a growing consciousness of others with whom to relate, is dominated even in those relationships by impulsive behaviour. Co-operative play with others is not possible, let alone rule-governed behaviour. None the less, such impulsive behaviour must be seen (in contrast with the pre-social stage) as an assertion of one's own separate existence as a person. The young child is very much concerned with the present and with him/herself, and fails to appreciate the more psychological dimensions of relationships.

Stage 3:   Self-protective

The impulsive behaviour gives way to rule-governed behaviour, with the growing realisation of these interpersonal rules and of where self-interest and self-protection lie in getting affection and rewards, or in avoiding punishment. This shift to 'rule-following' is crucial in the development of self, and it is reflected in a rather authoritarian conception of rules – as absolute, unchanging parts of the 'world' which it is in one's unquestionable self-interest to obey. Others are readily 'blamed' for breaking things, but not oneself, who (in protecting oneself against the personally damaging effect of being blamed) will always assert the accidental nature of one's own rule-breaking: hence, still very ego-centric (in fact a marvellous pen portrait of my six-year-old).

Stage 4:   Conformist

One's own self-interest becomes increasingly identified with that of the group and this in turn requires both the more subtle interpersonal qualities (for example, those of trust and loyalty) and the skills for maintaining these interpersonal relationships. The disapproval of those one finds significant is a most important sanction. Furthermore, if this occurs in a context devoid of interpersonal trust, then the child may remain at the self-protective stage. Of course, all this is rather messy at the boundaries. A growing person might identify with a relatively small social group of peers with whom there is a feeling of trust, and where there is respect for mutually agreed rules, but remain at the earlier 'self-protective' stage in relationship to others: school authorities, parents, the police. Development within this stage, therefore, lies in the gradual extension of the group with whom one does identify, reflected very often in that attempt to be helpful and to gain wider social approval.

Stage 5:   Conscientious

The stage of conformity may be where many remain; after all, so many social forces constrain one to remain at such a level. But an increasing self-awareness, an awareness of many competing values, and an awareness of the weaknesses in judgment and behaviour of those within one's group, become the pre-conditions for replacing group norms by greater self-questioning and self-evaluation. Judgment of present behaviour is determined less by the breaking of rules, and more by long term goals and consequences and by ascription of responsibility. There is a gradual establishment, through critical thinking and awareness, of one's own standards of behaviour.

Stage 6: *Autonomous*

Despite heightened 'conscientiousness' that overcomes unquestioned conformity there are still battles to be won, for there remains very often that inner conflict as well as the outer uncertainties. Decisions have to be made where no clear solution is available and where men of good disposition disagree amongst themselves. The capacity to acknowledge and live happily with this state of affairs, reflected in a tolerance of ideas different from one's own, indicates a degree of autonomy not very often achieved.

Such stage description does of course oversimplify a very complex set of changes, and there is so much more to be said about the interplay of growing self-awareness, rule-following behaviour, motives, reasoning powers, and emotions or feelings. But the account, even in this rather generalised form, picks out certain dominant features of different stages of childhood and adolescence, which need to be made more explicit and which, where acknowledged, affect how one might and indeed should relate as teacher to those in our charge. Let us consider briefly just some of these.

Firstly, such an account warns us against the rather simplistic view that all growth is a matter of self-actualisation. Such a notion might make sense at the later, conscientious, stages of development, but not earlier on where children need to learn how to control impulses, how to submit to and to internalise rules of behaviour, and how finally to engage critically with the prevailing values and assumptions of the people one lives and works with.

It should always be remembered, of course, that so much good teaching does precisely these things – forming, in the early years, trusting and stable environments where rules are established and impartially administered, and (in later years) the tools for self-reflection and for critical analysis (through the skillful teaching, say, of literature). But perhaps many teachers need to be more aware of these needs, lest development is left to chance. And perhaps, too, in the increasing demands upon tutors of adolescents in schools and in further education for training in social and life skills, we must be reminded that such training, if narrowly conceived, may miss the central requirements of trusting interpersonal relationships within the classroom and of the wider educational significance of increased critical awareness. Development can so easily end at clever self-protectionism or conformity.

Secondly, we need very often to shift the promotion of development from the stereotyped teaching role of instructing (especially in social and life skills) to that of facilitating development through creating the right kind of interpersonal relationships. How often are teaching goals in this area not attained through failure to establish the feelings of trust or because anxieties over discipline (or possibly personal insecurities on the part of the teacher) result in authoritarianism and an emphasis upon unquestioning conformity? This is a theme we must return to later.

5 Summary and Application

Development, as I said at the beginning of this chapter, is the sort of thing that parents and teachers are interested in when they ask how the things that children are doing or learning here and now relate to the achievement of desirable goals later on. Can one see a series of stages which, bit by bit, lead to the attainment of one's educational aims?

There are various ways in which one might conceptualise this connection between means and ends. The ones we have been considering might be crudely characterised as strong developmentalism, namely, that beneath the many surface behaviours are certain dominant structures of thinking or of behaving and that there is a definite sequential order in which one dominant structure is gradually transformed into more adequate and valuable ones. We also indicated that such a way of putting it is shot through with problems. None the less, there does seem to be considerable evidence to support such a general developmental picture, although it has its limitations, some of which we shall report in the next chapter. As teachers we therefore need to be aware of, first, the broad characterisation of this personal develop-

Piaget			Selman	Kohlberg	Loevinger
(a) practice of rules	(b) consciousness of rules	(c) types of morality	taking the perspective of the other	moral judgment	ego development
Regulations of behaviour (not rule-following strictly)	No conception of obligation		Ego-centric view-point	Oriented to rewards and avoiding punishment	Pre-social
Ego-centric approach to rules – imitative	Rules sacred and unchangeable	Heteronomy	Seeing others' viewpoints to be very like one's own	Oriented to instrumental values	Impulsive
Co-operative approach to rules			Accepting differences of viewpoint	Oriented to maintaining mutual expectation	Self-protective
	Rules changeable by mutual consent	Autonomy	Coming to terms with the equal validity of others' viewpoints	Oriented to a wider social perspective	Conformist
Codification of rules	Interest in rules 'per se' – as lawyers or moral philosophers		Generalising these acceptable differences to others and developing a group perspective	Oriented to individual rights beyond social norms	Conscientious
				Oriented to universal principles of justice	Autonomous

ment and, secondly, the implication of it for classroom-practice. Perhaps the chart (page 53) might distil the essence of what we have been talking about so far.

An even simpler characterisation of the development (see, for example, Garbarino and Bronfenbrenner, 1976) might be that of a gradual shift from the pre-social to the social stages (although the ways in which the pre-social and the social are manifested are legion, and the transition is gradual and always only more or less complete), and then from the social to the individualistic and autonomous. The earliest transition is that which needs to take place in early childhood; the second in middle and late adolescence. And the transition between stages depends upon the sort of socialisation permitted or encouraged by the social institutions the child or youngster belongs to (say, family, school, church). The general question therefore is clear enough: how to create the right kind of institutional and social settings and the right kinds of experience and relationship for these transitions to occur – or, at the least, for them not to be prevented from occurring?

NOTES

1   Longitudinal studies are those which study the same group of people as these people grow older. Obviously, therefore, it takes a long time for significant conclusions to be drawn from the studies about the relationship of what that group of people did at one age to what they did subsequently. Longitudinal studies are to be contrasted with those studies which, though comparing different ages, do so by obtaining a sample from different age groups at the same time. These have the advantage of speed but the disadvantages of comparing different groups of pupils, each pupil having his or her own individual history of development. Accounts by Kohlberg of his longitudinal study of moral development are to be found in his 1971a and 1976 papers. His more psychological papers have been collected together in Kohlberg (1983), Volume II. An invaluable philosophical reflection on his work is given in Kohlberg (1971b), and his philosophical papers have been collected together in Kohlberg (1981), Volume I. For an account of Kohlberg's work by others, see Peters (1971) and (1978), Weinreich-Haste (1983), and Hersh, Paolitto, and Reimer (1979). For a reservation that such broad categories of stage development might distract attention from individual differences, see Evans (1983).

2   This is an implicit reference to Rawls (1977). In his book *Theory of*

Justice, Rawls asks the reader to think of the kinds of rules that should regulate social life where these are devised 'from behind a veil of ignorance' about one's own circumstances – about, for instance, whether one will be intelligent or healthy or gifted. To imagine things from this point of view would ensure impartiality or fairness in the construction of rules, since one would propose those which would produce the best way of life not only for the community as a whole but also for the most disadvantaged within that community since, from one's position of ignorance, one does not know whether or not one will be amongst that group.

4 Moral Development

1 Morality as Rational Development

Can morals be taught? We would like to think so. It would be difficult for teachers or parents to accept that nothing they do can help to make children morally good. But there are difficulties in giving a positive answer.

We know what it means to teach mathematics or physics, for these are bodies of knowledge with their own concepts, principles and theories. We train people, moreover, to teach or to transmit such knowledge. But there is no such agreement about the nature of morality or about what makes a child good. As a result we do not, as Socrates pointed out in the *Meno*, appoint people to be teachers of virtue. In fact, it would seem a bit arrogant to claim to be a teacher of virtue or of morals, whereas it would not seem arrogant to claim to be a teacher of mathematics or physics.

We have, then, a paradox. On the one hand, the current concern for personal and social eduction has at its centre moral development, helping young people to be better persons (not better mathematicians or physicists). On the other hand, if there is no such thing as moral knowledge then 'it' cannot be taught and it cannot become part of an educational programme.

That there is no moral knowledge does, at first sight, seem correct. Even within our own society there is widespread disagreement about what is right or wrong in such matters as relations between the sexes, use of violence, obedience to authority, fiddling the books, stealing, racial harmony, pursuit of wealth. And between societies the differences are much greater. But the important thing is that there seems to be no rational way of sorting out these differences. Pointing to the facts of poverty does not seem relevant to deciding whether or not poverty should be tolerated (we are only too aware of the facts, but not too many people feel guilty about them). In the absence, therefore, of agreed procedures for settling moral disputes it is easy to conclude that there is no body of moral knowledge upon which the teacher can draw, and that therefore he or she has no authority to promote one view rather than another. Despite the importance attached to personal and social education, this must not, ironically, include the teaching of morals.

The underlying philosophical position has been outlined at length many times. One influential account (though there are many variations) is what is referred to as the emotive theory of ethics.[1] According to this view, we do make what appear to be moral judgments and we do engage in moral argument. Implicit in such judgments and arguments is the belief that what one is saying is true and that those who disagree are wrong. However, if there is no conceivable way of verifying what one is saying or of proving the conclusion of an argument (we simply do not know what would make it true), it is silly to assert something as though it were true. The so-called 'moral judgment' is not a proper or meaningful judgment at all, and arguing has no rational point.

What then, according to the theory, are we doing when we make what appear to be moral statements or engage in moral arguments? We are doing no more than expressing our feelings – although such expressions masquerade as claims to knowledge. For example, to say that the use of violence on a particular occasion is wrong is simply to express one's personal abhorence at the use of violence. It cannot be rationally argued that one 'view' is correct, and that the opposite is not, because there are no rational ways of justifying one claim against the other.

The philosophical view outlined here reflects a sceptical attitude towards 'moral knowledge' that has a profound effect upon any notion of moral, and thus implicitly personal and social, development. And yet it runs counter to what we strongly feel. For example, we are conscious within our lives of a 'moral struggle', that is, of trying to work out our moral duties on certain matters as though what is the right or the wrong thing to do is not simply a matter of feeling in the way that my liking for blackcurrant jam or for fell-walking is. The experience of obligation has a reference to standards that impose themselves upon me in a way that ordinary likes and dislikes don't. Can any sense be made of such feelings such that there may, after all, be a place for reason or knowledge in sorting out what I *ought* to do? And, if so, is there a place for moral *development* in so far as that capacity to reason develops?

One answer to this question lies in the attempt to distinguish between the form or structure of moral propositions and their content. We have introduced this distinction earlier in chapter 3. Roughly speaking the distinction is between the manner or way in which you think about moral matters (*how* you argue, the *kinds* of considerations that you take into account) and the particular views which you hold. Thus, by making such a distinction, one is able to say that two people holding quite different views (let us say, on pre-marital sex) might equally be considered moral because they hold their contradictory view after deliberations which have certain features in common. It is a matter not so much of *what* beliefs they hold but of *how* they hold them. Hence, moral development would consist in the changing way in which moral beliefs were held rather than in the acquisition of any specific behaviours or beliefs.

We would need, in upholding this distinction, to say much more about the form of moral judgment or belief. The philosopher Hare[2] characterised the form of moral judgments by reference to their function. They are essentially prescriptive. That is, we make moral statements, not to describe a state of affairs, but to *prescribe* a course of action. Furthermore the logic of prescriptive statements is that one gives reasons for or justifies any specific advice or prescription by appeal to more and more general principles, until ultimately it is not possible to get more general or to appeal further. Then one has arrived at one's ultimate principles, the ones that are overriding in one's life – the moral position which permeates so much of what one does. For example, if I choose not to take a shirt from a shop without paying, it may be because I believe that I ought not to steal. To say that I ought not to steal is to state a more general position which guides me in this and other particular circumstances. However, it can be argued, there is nothing distinctive about *me* which makes *my* stealing prohibited. I ought not to steal because stealing is wrong – not just for me but for others too. 'Thou shalt not steal' is a *principle* in that I am prepared to 'universalise' it, that is, make it applicable both to myself and to others on all like occasions. To break this principle would require reference to some higher level principle. For example, I may as a matter of principle believe that stealing is wrong. I may also believe that letting others suffer from hunger, when there is food around, is wrong. Furthermore, I may hold that where the two conflict, namely, where stealing is necessary for keeping someone from starving, the latter is the overriding principle. But to hold that means that I would be prepared to let someone steal from me should that be necessary to prevent someone dying of hunger.

'Prescriptivism', therefore, as this position has come to be called, asserts the essence of moral life to be that one lives according to principle, that is, that one works out, in view of the foreseeable consequences, what system of action-guiding rules one is prepared to subscribe to which would apply equally to oneself and to all others. Ultimately one's rules and the more general principles that encompass them are a matter of choice, but they are neither arbitrary nor whimsical, for they are what one is prepared to 'universalise' irrespective of how one's own or others' circumstances might change.

There are difficulties in this as an adequate account of 'being moral'. But it does point to certain features of moral life which must be respected in any account of moral development. Acting morally does require sticking to principles (and thus being consistent) rather than responding to moods and feelings and changing fashions. But to work out one's principles and to apply them requires thinking through the consequences of what one is prepared to do. It requires also being able to see things from another's point of view. Would I, for example, be able to subscribe to the principle 'one ought never to steal' if circumstances changed and I found myself in the position of someone in dire poverty surrounded by ostentatious wealth? To be a person of principle is to be contrasted with someone who simply serves his or her own interest; but that requires distancing oneself from one's own interest, seeing things from others' viewpoints, and adopting as far as possible a position of impartiality between different interests in coming to a decision.

Already we can see implications for the teaching of children – attitudes towards rule-following, the habit and ability to think through the consequences of the rules one is implicitly adopting, the imaginative insight into how others think and feel about things, perseverance in applying one's principles despite temptation and diversity. In a later section of this chapter I shall develop these implications further, but first I need to say more about *development* of this formal aspect.

Two related aspects need to be emphasised. Firstly, central importance is given to cognitive ability. Secondly, this ability is concerned with thinking things through in an impartial way. To that extent justice as fairness is seen as the central concept of morality. A moral action is one that flows impartially from a clear sense of duty that has been thought through according to first principles. And a moral person is one who is able, and tends, to think and act in this way. Moral development consists in getting children to acquire stage by stage this capacity to think in a more principled way about their practical life and eventually to adopt only those principles which can be universalised in a thoroughly fair and disinterested manner.

I have already outlined the stages in the development of moral judgment resulting from the work of Kohlberg. These stages could be seen in terms of the changing capacity of the child to think in terms of fairness. The very young child regards as unfair anything that does not fit in with his or her wishes. Only later is fairness connected with the application of rules. Even then the rules are fair or unfair depending upon how much they serve the young child's interest. Bit by bit the sense of impartiality between different interests is acquired. But it takes some time before the child can shift from requiring straight equality of treatment to the more equitable differentiation of treatment according to need or merit. Finally, of course, it is hoped that each person will reach the stage in which he or she will work out principles for distributing resources and for treating each other in a thoroughly disinterested manner – as though one was establishing rules and laws (and the distribution of resources and benefits) 'from behind a veil of ignorance' about one's own personal interests. In saying this Kohlberg makes reference to Rawl's theory of justice. It is the view of Kohlberg that if only we could get people to think formally in this thoroughly impartial way about their respective duties they would each arrive at a very similar moral content in most important matters. And this reflects the view of Hare (1973, page 164) where he says

> I am convinced that if parents first, and their children, understand better the formal character of morality and of the moral concept, there would be little need to bother, ultimately, about the content of our children's moral principles; for if the form is really and clearly understood, the content will look after itself.

There are three main reservations however about this as an adequate account of what being moral and what therefore moral development consists of. First, the weight is put upon the child learning to sort out his or her own principles. There is a stress upon 'autonomy' as though what is right or wrong is ultimately a matter of choice so long as one chooses in a certain sort of way. The subtitle of Mackie's (1977) book on ethics was 'Inventing right and wrong'. But it might be objected that morals have a content and that I live and think within a moral tradition which constrains what I might chose to universalise as my moral principles. That killing people is immoral, or that causing unnecessary pain to animals is wrong, is not open to negotiation in the way that my decision to devote my life to the care of the sick is. And if there is a moral content, then it might be argued this should be taught; it would not be enough to get children to develop the capacity for impartial reasoning and judgment. I shall examine this further in sections 2 and 3 below.

Secondly, the 'rational morality' as outlined stresses too much the action-guiding and rational nature of morality. Most of our recognisably moral life is conducted in a relatively unreflective and spontaneous way. We appraise people as kind, gentle, or modest, not because they have the right kind of principles but because they *feel* about people and situations in a certain sort of way. The place of feeling in moral development is terribly important, and this we shall examine in section 4.

Thirdly, it is objected that moral development is too closely linked with cognitive ability, whereas moral appraisal is concerned as much with what we *do* as with how we think about it. Parents want their children not to steal and not to hit each other; they want them to be polite and to do kind acts. They do not want them simply to be very astute in *thinking* about what they ought to do. What then is the connection between thinking and doing? To one answer to this problem we turn immediately.

2   Morality as Behaving Correctly

A major worry about the 'rational morality' referred to previously is that it puts the whole moral force upon the quality of a person's *thinking*. Therefore, only those who have reached the higher level of moral thinking can be fully moral. And this runs counter to the stress so often put, in our concerns about the moral upbringing of children, upon the right kind of *behaviour*. We are more worried about what they *do* than about what they *think* – and we punish accordingly. However, the connection between thought and action is not straightforward: we cannot be sure children will behave as we want them to as a result of our teaching them to think 'correctly'. (The research literature on the connection between moral thought and moral action is thoroughly summarised by Blasi (1980); this supports the view that higher stages of moral reasoning are predictive of moral behaviour but the connections are not easy to conceptualise, particularly what is meant by 'consistency'.)

It is not surprising therefore that an alternative approach to moral development stresses behaviour, not as something which might or might not follow from principled thinking (depending upon the strength of will), but as something to be trained or altered in itself. Obvious examples of this are various programmes of behaviour modification.

On this view, according to Poteet (1973, page 7), 'behaviour is what someone does that we can see'. All the things that children do (or what we as teachers or parents want them to do) could be described in terms of what you can observe without any reference to the intention or principles or other unobservable 'mental acts' which so often befog discussion of moral development. What moral education is chiefly about is changing behaviour and 'behaviour' refers to all physical acts that children perform. Thus, for example (to quote Poteet, page 7)

> Take the student who is often out of his seat. Here we are concerned with 'out-of-seat' behaviour. Wolf and others defined such behaviour as 'the seat portion of the child's body is not in contact with any part of the seat of the child's chair'.

As Poteet then points out 'This is a clever and useful definition'. It would enable us to treat changing behaviour (which for many lies at the centre of 'moral development') in a very scientific way, which of course is what the behaviourists do.

The truth contained in this view needs to be acknowledged. To ignore the physical consequences of one's actions as something totally irrelevant to their moral appraisal would be silly. There does seem to be a certain 'moral content'. But to isolate the purely physical aspects and consequences of what people do from how they think or feel about it would seem equally untenable. To *understand* what people do requires some reference to how they see their actions and to their intentions and, as Piaget pointed out (see page 37), the transition in appraising an action, from judging according to physical consequences to judging according to intentions, is a gradual but vital one. To change behaviour, therefore, without reference to how the pupil understands what he is doing, has got little to do with *moral* development. An orderly, well-disciplined school, whose members go through the motions of polite behaviour, might have done very little for the moral education of the pupils; their general intentions and motives may be of a singularly selfish kind and their respect for the needs of others quite immature.[3]

So often investigations into the moral development of young children have failed to take their intentions sufficiently into account. For example, the oft quoted study of honesty conducted by Hartshorne and May (1928) indicated that on thirty-three different tests of dishonesty (embracing instances of cheating, stealing, and lying) there was very little correlation between the results of each test or between the test results and the pupils' general statements of honesty. This seemed to be evidence against the view that the pupils acted on general principles – their behaviours were specific to particular situations. And the conclusions easily drawn from such a study would be that, instead of instilling general principles into children, we ought instead to be modifying specific behaviour in specific contexts. However, the Hartshorne and May experiment measured 'conduct' which was defined without any reference to how the pupils saw their actions. What appeared to the experimenter to be cheating would not have been so if the examinee had not seen it as such, and there might have been more consistently honest behaviour if we had known more about the intentions and the points of view of the pupils. Cheating is not something you 'observe' in the absence of an interpretation of the pupils' understanding of the situation.

A problem, therefore, lies in a quite indefensible definition of 'good behaviour' which many teachers and parents implicitly hold, namely one in which the intentions, motives, reasons, and feelings of the children play little part in judgments made about their behaviour or in plans to improve it. But in this there is considerable confusion. It is not logically possible to make sense of human actions without reference to the actor's intentions. The physical act of raising my hand *could* be that of stretching or of seeking attention or of signalling to a friend or of waving goodbye– depending on what my intentions are. And the moral appraisal of what I do would need to refer to those intentions, and to the underlying principles.

This, however, presents those interested in moral education with a difficulty. On the one hand, as I have argued in section 1, theoretical accounts of moral action that concentrate upon moral reasoning seem to have little to say about behaviour (although see Blasi, 1980, for a summary of the research evidence on this). On the other hand, it seems equally mistaken to talk of moral behaviour without reference to what 'went on inside my head', the intentions, quality of reasoning, and so on. How can we reconcile the two?

3   Moral Content

One way of expressing the problem so far outlined is this. To identify moral development with the quality or mode of reasoning is tantamount to saying that there is no *content* to morality, no facts about what is right or wrong to be taught or to be discovered. Teachers must teach their pupils *how* to think but not *what* to think. At the other extreme there are those who would stress moral content or right behaviour; but, in doing so, they miss that which gives behaviour its distinctively moral quality, namely the kind of intentions, motives, and reasoning that lie behind it.

That there is a content to morality would, however, seem to be the case. What is the right thing to do is not just a matter of choice or of personal decision. Hurting people for the sake of it, telling lies whenever it is personally convenient to do so, habitually breaking promises, all seem to be wrong. But the status of that 'content' can be understood in two different ways. First, content could refer to what is considered right or wrong within a particular social tradition, bearing in mind that 'content' changes from society to society. Thus, the content of Roman Catholic, but not of humanistic, morality is that abortion is wrong; some schools, but not others, place a lot of moral value upon obedience to and respect for authority.

Secondly, content could refer to those actions which are considered right or wrong independently of any particular social tradition. To believe in moral content in this second sense puts an obligation upon the moral education to make accessible to young people a set of values and obligations which transcend social boundaries – and it puts an obligation upon the learner to find out, often through considerable reflection and personal struggle, what he or she ought to do, independently of what society says should be done. Perhaps content, understood in this latter sense, needs to be expressed fairly abstractly and generally and thus is open to different interpretations in different social contexts, but content it is. Moral content, however viewed, is to be contrasted with the belief that right and wrong are created or invented by the individual person (see Mackie, 1977) and that the *sole* determinant of moral quality is the quality of the reasoning or feeling with which the behaviour is invested.

Most people implicitly believe that there is a content to morality in the second sense, although they would find it difficult to justify that content. They have been brought up to believe that certain actions are prohibited, others permitted. Furthermore, if it was objected that such obligations and rights vary from group to group (thus undermining the belief that there is a content which transcends social boundaries and which is not ultimately the invention of particular people), it could be argued that such apparent differences are by and large adaptations of more fundamental principles to specific social contexts. And there is a respectable philosophical tradition from Plato onwards which would support such a view. Certain things are good and others bad, and you either *see* that or you don't. If you don't see it, then you are morally blind (just as those who do not see that the pen I am holding is red are colour blind).[4]

The general rules of action which form the content of morality would include such things as treating other people with respect, not causing unnecessary hurt or pain, taking seriously other people's interests, telling the truth, and keeping promises. It would be difficult to conceive a morality that did not subscribe in some way to such principles – although what counts as being in the interests of others, or who should be included in the category of 'persons' (see pages 12–14), or where to place the outer boundaries of truth telling and promise keeping, may change radically from society to society.

Within particular societies such general principles would be reflected in fairly specific rules and values, and in social customs and laws; and indeed this is how they would need to be taught. To give an almost trivial example, to say 'please' when asking for something is to follow a particular convention within our society. One can easily imagine social groups where such a convention is not treated seriously – there is no overwhelming reason why it should be. But the significance of 'please' lies in its expression of a certain attitude towards the other person. It is a conventional way of showing respect, and the value of respect is both taught and recognised through the adoption of this particular convention. The content of morality therefore will consist at one level of fairly general principles, and at another level of specific rules and conventions which, it is hoped, will reflect these principles. The more general principles are implicit within the particular rules, and are acquired through being taught these rules. And moral development will lie therefore in acquiring the moral conventions – the do's and don't's of a society – in such a way that the youngster will come to see the more general principles which lie behind rules.

The consequence of this for the parent or teacher is two-fold. First, it is important to identify, and then to examine critically, those rules or conventions which we impose upon young people. Can we justify them either because of the practical benefits they provide (such as ensuring safety within the school or efficient distribution of resources) or because of the more general principles which they reflect and which constitute the content of morality? So often young people are subject to rules and regulations (about dress, say, or about where they can or cannot go), which cannot be defended either practically or morally.

Secondly, it is important to help young people to see the reasons behind the rules, that is the more general principles which they are supposed to reflect. Of course, if we are to believe Piaget, this can be achieved only at certain stages of development. The very young child needs to be taught the rules – full stop. But as often, and as soon, as possible the justification for these rules in terms of the general principle they reflect should be provided. That, however, can be done only where there *are* general principles behind the rules and where the teacher or parent recognises them.

The education of young people, whether in the personal and moral area or not, needs to respect where they are – the way *they* understand and think about things. Otherwise it is difficult to see how *they* are being educated. It is significant therefore that two fairly recent investigations into the moral development of young people have started with an enquiry into the values, that is the do's and don'ts, that young people hold – the content of *their* morality. First, the Schools Council Project *Moral Education 13 to 16* started with an enquiry into what adolescent boys and girls thought moral education to be. The vast majority stressed the consideration of the needs, interests and feelings of others and, in the light of such general moral content, the right and freedom to challenge the 'traditionally respected adult sets of values and beliefs' (see

McPhail *et al.*, 1972, pages 35 and 37). Furthermore, these considerations arose most significantly in the interpersonal relationships between people, and one barrier to such relationships lay in the failure of confidence in their own identity. As a result of these initial findings, the Project felt that moral education should focus upon such day to day concerns of the young and help develop what was referred to as a 'morality of communication'.

Secondly, Kitwood (1980) investigated the values which underpinned the actions of young people and were 'real' to them. Moral education should not assume that even those who, on the surface, seem to live amoral lives have no moral values. Nor should it assume therefore that one can instruct young people in a moral content as though their minds are moral blanks, waiting to be filled. On the other hand, to get at the tacit values that do underpin the young person's behaviour requires a relationship of trust and of openness that is all too rarely achieved. Hence, the significance of the long preparatory work, the involvement in the adolescents' world, and the open-ended questioning which characterised Kitwood's investigations. How can you get young people to 'disclose themselves to a stranger'?

There are fairly obvious objections to these procedures if they are wrongly interpreted. First, it may be argued that no empirical investigation into what adolescents value entails anything about what they *should* value. The actual content of morality may not be the 'proper' content of morality – that which needs to be taught in schools. Secondly, the concerns of young people for respecting others' needs and interests sound fine when expressed so generally. But these general principles need to be translated into the complexity of everyday life, and therein lies so often the moral difficulty – being sensitive to and interpreting the interests and needs of others. Thirdly, we have seen from developmental psychology the qualitatively different ways in which people are able to think about, and to respond to, the needs of others. And the way in which many young people 'consider the needs, interests and feelings of others' may be open to qualitative improvement.

These difficulties are not criticisms of the Schools Council Project or of Kitwood. Far from it. Both the project and Kitwood, quite rightly, point to the overriding importance of respecting, and starting from, where young people are and of taking steps to find out what *they* value and how *they* feel. Rather do these difficulties constitute objections to any moral education which accepts what young people value as necessarily indicative of what, objectively speaking, is valuable. As teachers we must try to lead young people from where they are to what can be shown to be a more adequate, improved way of seeing and feeling about things. But one must begin with where the young people are and one must respect the insights and the feelings that they have. Otherwise, the moral education so-called will neither respect nor affect them as persons.

One final point on moral content is this. I have been talking about the kinds of principles, and the rules that, in a particular social group, embody those principles which need to be taught. But to learn to act morally, a person needs to be able to see things from a moral point of view and thus to have a grasp of those moral concepts and modes of moral reasoning which enable him to do this. I am not thinking simply of the grand concept of 'duty', 'ought' or 'right'. The concepts through which we come to think about things and to experience relationships in moral terms are many and complex, and enter into the fabric of our language in all sorts of subtle ways. The language of morality – of motive, of appraisal, of values – needs to be learnt, and to some extent learnt simply by gaining mastery of the English language and through reading a literature which explores moral issues.

Wilson (1972 and 1973), however, argues for a more systematic approach to becoming familiar with moral language – the concepts, and the skills of moral reasoning – than that. He talks of acquiring the correct methodology of the 'subject'. More of this in section 6 (iii).

4   Moral Dispositions

As I have indicated, a lot of work in moral education has focused upon moral reasoning. The connection between reasoning and behaviour, however, is not so clear, and therefore there is the temptation to concentrate instead upon modifying behaviour.

There are two aspects of this connection that I want to consider here, although there is much more to be said in chapter 5. First, the connecting link between what reason says I should do and what I do in fact do must lie in some feeling or disposition to act according to practical reason. There must be some sense of obligation, of duty. Secondly, however, this approach to moral development – the concentration upon reasoning and obligation –

might seem rather one-sided, omitting reference, as it does, to the range of feelings which are part of the moral life.

At the beginning of *The Republic*, Thrasymachus asks Socrates, why be moral? It is a 'Catch 22' question. If one gives a moral answer for being moral, then the question is begged. If one gives a non-moral answer for being moral (such as moral people generally prosper), then the subsequent 'moral' behaviour is no longer moral – it simply has the appearance of morality. The point is that, in the absence of a certain inclination to take moral considerations seriously, moral reasons will not be reasons for *action*.

The philosopher Kant considered the moral life to be one in which one acted out of a sense of duty. And this was to be contrasted with acting according to one's feelings which were not subject to the control of reason and which could be rather wayward. The good person was he or she who pursued what, according to practical reasoning, could be universalised, that is, made into a general principle, applicable to everyone, including oneself, in like circumstances. But, although the 'good will' of Kant was to be contrasted with a life lived at the level of feeling only, it required at least one elementary 'feeling', namely the *sense* of duty or the respect for what practical reason said should be the case. What can be said about the origin and development of this sense of principle or of duty?

Wright (1982) describes how this might be explained by drawing upon Piaget's (1932) *Moral Judgment of the Child*. The problem is put on page 410 as follows:

> For conduct to be characterised as moral there must be something more than an outward agreement between its content and that of commonly accepted rules: *it is also requisite that the mind should tend towards morality as to an autonomous good and should itself be capable of appreciating the value of the rules that are proposed to it.*

Not only, then, must one have the ability to go through the motions, as it were, of formulating moral rules of action (one's duties or obligations) but also one must apprehend them as worthy of acting on. That is, one must apprehend these rules as having their own particular attractions simply because they are seen as moral rules. Seeing a course of action as a duty, and feeling that one ought to pursue it, are, in one sense, one and the same thing. But how can one explain the development of this continuation of seeing and feeling that constitutes the mature moral person?

Central to Piaget's explanation is the social context in which any system of rules, and adoption of those rules, must be understood. From the beginning the child lives a form of social life which is defined and regulated by a set of rules. These enter necessarily into the relationships which the child is part of. The rules that govern these relationships and define the form of social life are, of course, beneath the surface of consciousness, but they are implicitly submitted to in the allegiance that the child pays to his or her relationships. The more conscious realisation of these rules, as the child grows older, will not rid him of the allegiance to them but only make them the occasional focus of reflection, especially where there is a conflict between these and other tendencies. At the initial stages of this conscious realisation of the rules, the continued allegiance to them will be characterised by unilateral respect for those within the social context who appear to be either originators or arbiters of the rules. However, with the gradual shift, in the right conditions, from unilateral towards mutual respect for others, the 'tendency' will remain towards those rules as worthy of allegiance in so far as they are seen to constitute and maintain the social relationships.

None the less, moral life, depicted as the continual fulfilment of one's duty, does appear rather stark and forbidding. For Kant, virtue lay in the moral struggle. Fortunate, therefore, was the person with strong inclinations that run counter to the sense of duty, for in the victory over those inclinations lay the moral victory.

One could, however, look at the moral struggle from a quite different point of view. The good man would be he who 'naturally' did what he ought to do. The sense of obligation rarely arises – in fact, it would be an indication of moral weakness rather than of moral strength if someone were to engage in charitable acts or to keep promises 'out of a sense of obligation'. Rather is the good person he or she who has the appropriate feelings or the dispositions to do good things. People are described as kind who have a general inclination to act kindly. Moral development would consist therefore in acquiring those feelings or dispositions to act in particular ways in appropriate situations – the virtues of kindness, humility, modesty, generosity, tolerance, and so on. Any list of virtues would indicate the kinds of quality that a particular society values and wants to appraise people by. And these would, of course, change – the Greeks valued magnanimity, but this would not figure in most Englishmen's list of virtues.

The implications for this educationally are quite considerable. One is, as teacher or parent, concerned with developing not simply a sense of obligation and a capacity to think things through in a principled way, but also those feelings which are valued within the social group one belongs to. Many of those moral virtues (such as loyalty and honesty) will, in one way or another, be valued across social boundaries. But others will be peculiar to only a minority – for example, the respect for honour that is so important in Japanese society. In chapter 2, section 3, I distinguished between different kinds of dispositions – intellectual, moral, character traits. I shall not repeat the argument here, but once one agrees that feelings, tendencies, and inclinations are an important part of moral life, then one needs to address oneself to some systematic analysis of them.

One feeling, however, stands out particularly as the key to all the others, namely that of altruism or the inclination to care for, or to be concerned about, what happens to others. In the accounts given so far altruism has played an important part. And this is quite understandable, since it would be difficult to make sense of such virtues as kindness, generosity, respect for others, or loyalty, unless there was some underpinning quality of altruism.

How then does an altruistic disposition towards others arise? Is it not really a disguised form of selfishness, and thus to be explained as a way of achieving one's own ends? Hoffman (1975) argues for a developmental account of how this disposition arises quite independently of egoistic or self-rewarding motives. First, people of all ages instinctively, on some occasions at least, tend to help others in distress even where there is no benefit for them in doing so. Secondly, this tendency is connected with a basic 'affective reaction to another's feelings'. Indeed it would seem that the involuntary experiences of another person's painful emotional state happen very early, even before there is any cognitive awareness of the other as a person (Simner, 1971). Thirdly, however, since the nature of this affective response will depend upon how one understand or appreciates 'another's feelings', the development of altruism will depend upon the interaction between the basic empathic response and the changing understanding of the other person.

Hoffman delineates the broad stages in this development which, needless to say, relate closely to the developmental theories we have already examined. First, the young child acquires the sense of the other existing as a separate physical entity. Secondly, she gradually acquires the sense of the other's inner state being different from her own, and this is demonstrated even at an early age through imaginative role play. Thirdly, the child comes to see the other as having a personal identity and life beyond the immediate situation. These developmental stages affect the nature of the empathic response to others in distress and therefore how altruistic tendencies arise from the early confusion of another person's distress with one's own (and thus to be assuaged in exactly the same way), to an increased sensitivity in understanding how different people need one's help, to an appreciation of the deeper significance of the distress signals and thus of the kind of relationship that is required.

This, of course, is all too brief an account of such an important philosophical and educational territory. What needs to be remembered, however, by the educator is that those concerned with personal and moral education need, despite the emphasis in the literature to the contrary, to attend to the development of feelings as much as to the development of reason. Aspects of this development are: respect for thinking and acting according to principles, transforming that very elementary response to others' distress into a sympathetic appreciation of their needs, and the acquisition of those dispositions to be kind, modest, loyal and so on which we value in people.

5   Autonomy

Implicit in a lot of the research and literature I have referred to is the ideal of autonomy as the ultimate aim of personal, social, and moral education. In other literature this is quite explicit (Dearden, 1972, Peters, 1981).

Autonomy will of course mean different things to different people. But one major distinction needs to be made at once. Autonomy in the first sense refers to the ability to make up one's own mind about what is right or wrong. It is contrasted with the dependence of people upon authority. Thus autonomous persons have freely adopted those principles of behaviour, which, after due thought, they believe to be appropriate, rather than remain, unreflectively, within the particular moral tradition in which they have been brought up. Secondly, however, autonomy refers to the ability to stick to those principles, not requiring the social props that weaker mortals require to keep them on the straight and narrow path of virtue they have freely chosen. Put crudely, autonomy can refer either to the quality of thinking or to the quality of the will to do what one thinks one ought to do.

In Piaget and Kohlberg, referred to earlier, autonomy in the first sense is a transformation of, and thus is *necessarily* preceded by, that state of heteronomy in which a person lives according to values and rules of behaviour prescribed, not by himself, but by others – parents, church, or social agencies of one kind or another. The state of autonomy, being a transformation of the earlier non-autonomous stage of development, is thereby superior and to be promoted as the end of moral growth.

There are, however, worrying features about too careless a use of this notion. These worries concern the exaggerated stress upon individualism that is so often associated with the achievement of autonomy, and the neglect of the social nature and context in which one develops as a person. Erick Fromm (1942) did, in *The Fear of Freedom*, point to the psychological difficulties that arise from a commitment to autonomy which ignores the essentially social traditions in which one lives and grows as a person. True, the autonomous person is he who 'makes his own' the principles which are to guide personal decisions, but these principles, and a person's ability to examine and to adopt them, arise out of a social tradition of thinking and of criticising which we each, in our separate ways, belong to. There needs to be a respect for the moral authority of that tradition, even if as a result of subsequent thought and reflection one adapts it in various ways.

To make these difficulties clear, let us attend briefly to the different senses in which autonomy is referred to in personal and moral development.[5] First, there is the sense of autonomy in which each individual sorts out *for himself* what is right or wrong, as though there is no moral content to be learnt or moral tradition to be obeyed. Such a position, associated as I pointed out earlier with Mackie (1977) and Hare (1952 and 1963) seems mistaken. There *is* a moral content (we cannot, for example, tolerate with indifference racism in pupils however autonomously they have prescribed such values for themselves) and, in experiencing the moral life, we measure our behaviour against standards that are not of our own creation.

Secondly, there is the sense of autonomy where it means 'independence of authority'. This, however, can be understood in either a strong or a weak sense. In the strong sense it would mean simply ignoring those with wider experience of the tradition of moral values one has inherited. That for any individual is unwise since the moral life is too complex for any one individual to work everything out from scratch. In the weaker sense, however, autonomy would mean an initial respect for authority – a readiness to listen – but an increasingly critical attitude towards it as one tries to understand the principles that lie behind the authoritative utterance.

A third sense of autonomy refers to having a consistent and integrated set of values that are defensible and that are truly one's own. The values, and the integrated sense of purpose that go with them, are thoroughly assimilated. They don't get overruled at the next change of fashion or when one is under pressure. Autonomy in this third sense is indeed compatible with a respect for tradition and for authority, but it requires a capacity for reflective and critical thinking at the higher stages of development referred to by Piaget and Kohlberg, if it is to be sustained in a rather complex world where the individual is confronted with so many contradictory points of view.

A fourth but connected meaning of autonomy refers to the sense of personal identity (what Loevinger referred to as ego strength; see pages 47–51). Here one has a sufficiently strong sense of one's own distinct identity as a person, of one's own value, and of one's sense of purpose in life, that one is not sent hither and thither by wayward feelings or changing fashions, nor easily smothered by personal pressures. It is a matter of 'where id was there ego shall be' – and with not too much superego either.

These brief remarks are important because autonomy is seen too easily to be the aim of personal and social education without analysis of what it means. As a result it is too often thoughtlessly identified with, first, a freedom from authority and traditional values which ignores the complexity of moral life that a young person needs to come to terms with and, secondly, an individual self-determination that can rarely be sustained. When autonomy is so narrowly interpreted, one could argue that the world would be a happier place if there were fewer autonomous people making decisions about what is good or bad and that, since happiness and dignity are supremely important, we want to ensure that our children acquire those virtues and moral habits which will make the world a happier place to live in.

What need to be brought out, however, are: (i) an attitude to authority and to 'taken for granted rules' that, though respectful

of them, becomes increasingly questioning of the principles behind the rules; (ii) an increasing integration of the values and
purposes that permeate one's actions and relationships; and (iii) a
sense of one's own value and identity through different circumstances and pressures.

6   Moral Education in Practice

In the light of these sections, I want to refer briefly to examples of
curriculum practice.

(i)   Values Clarification

In section 1 I outlined one philosophical position which cast doubt
upon the objectivity, indeed the intelligibility, of moral judgments, and this scepticism permeates a lot of education thinking
about moral development. After all, if there is no objective basis
for saying that certain values or ways of life are better than others,
then there is no defensible body of knowledge upon which to draw
in order to teach.

One influential consequence of this, especially in North
America, has been that of values clarification. If one cannot say
what pupils should do, then at least one can help them to clarify
their values and to make up their own minds. Key people here are
Simon (1972) and Rath (1966). The premise is that children ought
to be free to choose and to create their own values. The strategy for
doing this might be roughly summarised as follows:

(a)   to choose what one should do
      – freely;
      – having identified the alternative courses of action; and
      – having considered thoughtfully the consequences of each
        alternative;
(b)   to prize or value what one has chosen sufficiently to be willing
      to justify convincingly one's evaluation to others;
(c)   to act upon the choice, not just once but repeatedly, as
      though it were to become part of one's life pattern.

Note, of course, that there are certain values that are presupposed here and are not to be freely chosen, namely, those of
freedom to choose. This is the supreme value of value clarifica-

tion but one (as I implied in my account of autonomy) which needs to be questioned. An excellent critique of values clarification in which the philosophical presuppositions are questioned, along lines similar to those in this chapter, is that of Gow (1980).

To identify values clarification, therefore, with moral education would be wrong. It would, however, be equally wrong to dismiss it, and its very practical teaching strategies, from moral education. Personal growth, and the achievement of autonomy in the more acceptable sense referred to, does require a clarification of where one stands on various issues and a clarification, too, of the alternative solutions to the moral issues one is confronted with. Any teaching strategy is welcome that helps with this, so long as it does not give the impression that there is no content to morality which needs to be learnt and to be respected.

(ii)   Workshops in Values Education

Kohlberg's hypothetical dilemmas were used essentially for research purposes. The *Scoring Manual* (see Colby *et al.*, 1983b) is a very sophisticated instrument for assessing the competence at different, well-defined levels of moral judgment.

The research, however, raises the question of how this development in competence might be promoted. Fenton's and Kohlberg's (1976a) published workshop on teacher training in values education was one answer to this.[6] They argued that, by exposing young people to these dilemmas in a systematic and regular way and by encouraging them in groups to discuss the appropriate action and the reasons for choosing that action, a teacher could achieve a measurable development of the moral reasoning of the young person. The sort of classroom approach that I have tried, following this work, is as follows:

Plenary session
(a)   obtain from the class the meaning and significance of moral dilemmas, the conflict between two fundamental values and the need to weigh up the relevance of different reasons;
(b)   tell a story which illustrates a dilemma;
(c)   clarification;
(d)   initial response: (i)   should he/she do x? (vote taken)
                                      (ii)   give the main reason.

Group discussion aimed at reconciling different decisions and reasons.

Plenary session where, in the light of the group discussions, the vote is retaken and reasons explained.

One dilemma, taken from Kohlberg's research, is as follows (it can easily be adapted to suit the class needs, and both teacher and pupils might think up other 'real life' dilemmas):

A widow was near death from a particularly severe form of cancer. There was one drug that might save her. A druggist in town had recently developed it, and it was still in the experimental stages. The drug was expensive to make, but the druggist still charged ten times what it cost him. He paid $200 for the ingredients and charged $2,000 for enough of the drug to cure a patient.

The widow had no children and no close family in the town. Her neighbours, Mr and Mrs Heinz, knew her but she was not one of their closest friends. It soon became clear however that no one else would help her. The Heinzes were poor and could get together only half of the $2,000 it took to buy the drug. The druggist refused to lower his price, claiming that he had worked hard for many years to invent the drug and deserved to make money from it. But without the drug, the widow seemed sure to die.

Question: Should Heinz steal the drug to save the dying woman? Why or why not?

The theoretical background to this classroom practice is as follows. The quality of children's moral thinking changes so that, if you probe beneath the surface answers, you will find that there are characteristic ways of reasoning about moral matters. This is reflected particularly in their handling of questions of fairness or of justice, which seems fundamental to most moral judgments. At an early stage, for example, what is fair or unfair will relate very much to their own self-interest. Later they will be able to see things in terms of objective values although these values will be embedded in the conventions of their own social group. Only much later will they develop the capacity for thinking in terms of universal principles in the light of which they can criticise received values.

The main purpose of this exercise is two-fold:

1   to encourage children, through discussion and reasoning

about moral dilemmas, to develop the capacity to consider issues in a qualitatively superior way;

2   to help the teacher to probe more deeply the deeper structure of children's moral thinking.

This approach, again, has its limitations. Its achievements lie in more sophisticated thinking about hypothetical dilemmas, and these are by no means to be discounted because increased competence here is an important component of moral development. But it is only a component. The transfer of this competence to real dilemmas, and away from the 'laboratory conditions' of the classroom, has still to be shown. That seems to some extent an act of faith – although that hardly puts it into a different league from the other things we do in schools. Furthermore, it can run into political problems. A description of this approach in the Devon (1982) publication on personal, social, and moral education, provoked a 'disturbed' response from the *Western Morning News*, 23 September 1982. The content, not the form, of moral belief was, according to this critic, of paramount importance.

(iii)   Farmington Trust

Perhaps the best known analysis of moral education in Britain is that of the Farmington Trust.[7] In Wilson, Williams, and Sugarman (1967), and subsequently, in Wilson (1969), (1972) and (1973), the concept is analysed and the contribution of psychology and sociology to its development spelt out. The gist of the argument might be summarised as follows. Just as doing science is a matter not simply of learning scientific statements but also of adopting them critically and of knowing how to pursue scientific principles, getting at the truth of things, so too morals are not just a matter of acquiring moral 'knowledge' but also of 'doing' morality, of thinking out what one ought to do *in a certain way* and of coming to decisions that are morally defensible and that one is prepared to stick by. Morality is a matter of rule-following, but what makes the rules moral rules is that they are (1) prescriptive; (2) overriding (and not just prudential); (3) concerned with others' interests; (4) freely adopted (as opposed to being adopted as a result of compulsion or unthinkingly); (5) rational (in the sense that reasons can be given); (6) impartial as between persons.

For curriculum purposes, Wilson analysed the components of the morally educated person as follows. (See Wilson, Williams and

Sugarman, 1967, page 192 or Wilson, 1969, page 2, although a more refined list is to be found in Ward, 1983, page 130.)

PHIL   –   having a concept of, and an attitude of respect towards, others as persons;

EMP   –   having an understanding of how others think and feel;

GIG   –   knowing other facts relevant to practical decisions in relation to other people;

DIK   –   formulating a system of values or prescriptions as a result of PHIL, EMP, and GIG;

PHRON –   relating these formulations to oneself, who needs to be valued;

KRAT   –   translating these principles into practice.

The analysis of the components of moral education in this way provides a useful check-list and might be useful objectives for teaching purposes. We do need, for example, to ensure that this awareness of and respect for others as persons (PHIL) is achieved through the normal life of the school. Or again, EMP focuses our attention upon the need for role play and simulation exercises, already referred to in the course of this book, as means for gaining insight into the feelings of others. In his 1973 book, Wilson also provides ways in which the teacher can help young people to formulate these different considerations into rules of action.

The Farmington Trust's work was a notable landmark in the development of moral education theory and practice. There are three possible criticisms however. First, the developmental understanding of impartiality and of rule-following, that Kohlberg in particular sensitised us to, requires much greater emphasis. Secondly, the stress upon competence at thinking things through for oneself ignores the importance of the content of moral tradition, which needs to be respected. Thirdly, the rather rational approach pays insufficient attention to the place of feeling and to the development of dispositions which I referred to in section 4.

(iv)   Schools Council Project *Moral Education 13 to 16*[8]

This Project commenced in 1967, and is reported in McPhail, Ungoed-Thomas, and Chapman (1972). Its main task was to design, test, and develop curriculum material to help secondary school children find and adopt 'better' solutions to interpersonal problems. As explained in section 3, it started with a small-scale

enquiry into what adolescent boys and girls thought moral education should be about. From the start the questions were slanted so
as to evoke responses concerned with the quality and problems of
interpersonal relations. The young people were particularly critical of instruction about interpersonal relations that was not
reflected in the practice of the school and teachers. Also considerable anxieties, affecting the quality of relationships, were expressed about establishing their own identities as persons. Indeed, 70
per cent of the pupils insisted that the school should devote more
of its time to offering practical help and support in their search for
solutions to interpersonal problems. It was concluded therefore
that any programme of moral education that focused on the
quality of interpersonal relations needed to respect and to start
from the present experiences and active day-to-day concerns of the
young people.

To do this, however, required a closer examination of the needs
and concerns of adolescents. A wider sample for enquiry was then
chosen and each was asked to answer two critical questions: 'Give
me one example if you can of a situation in which you think an
adult treated you well' and 'Give one example if you can of a
situation in which you think an adult treated you badly'. An added
'critical incident' question was asked of some: 'Tell me about a
time when you found a situation difficult to respond to, or did not
know what to do'. What emerged was a deep concern that others'
needs, feelings, and interests should be (but frequently were not)
taken into account and that schools should be actively involved in
supporting this at what McPhail referred to as 'the age of social
experiment'. From these considerations emerged the project's
'Lifeline' programme which aimed at helping boys and girls to
develop a 'considerate style of life'. The general strategy was
initially to use problems provided by pupils but to place these
problems increasingly in contexts familiar to pupils in which they
must find their own solutions. This was achieved through a variety
of methods: discussion, role play, simulation exercises, art –
whatever encouraged an emotional as well as a rational response.
There were three kinds of materials to help achieve this:

(1)   *In Other Peoples' Shoes*
(2)   *Proving the Rule*
(3)   *What would you have done?*

This project was an implicit criticism of those moral education
programmes which treated the problems too didactically, as

though there was no difficulty in harnessing the emotions of the young people themselves. Such feelings and personal concerns, however, cannot be ignored, and McPhail placed these, and the systematic reflection upon problems connected with those feelings, at the centre of the curriculum response. But it was pointed out that the systematic use of materials would be of little avail if the quality of relationships within school and classroom were not consonant with the major aims of the programme.

(v) Schools Council Project *Moral Education 8 to 13*

A similar approach was adopted in the project concerned with a younger age range. Once again, it was felt to be important that moral education should begin from where the children are – their reports 'about the moral situation, or culture, in which they found themselves'. Indeed, in explaining such a beginning Ungoed-Thomas (1978, page 3) states:

> The team considered that, without an insight into the moral world of children, it would be difficult, if not impossible, to design educational materials which would be motivating, relevant and appropriate.

The questions asked of the children were primarily concerned 'with the behaviour of the individual in relation to other individuals and with the happiness (or unhappiness) of the individual' (Ungoed-Thomas, 1978, page 25). And this general orientation was defended as being of central importance in the codes of behaviour of most moral traditions. The questions were:

(1) Write and draw about a time when somebody made you feel pleased or happy.
Describe what you did as a result.

(2) Write and draw about a time when somebody made you feel frightened, angry or unhappy.
Describe what you did as a result.

(3) Write and draw about a time when you were with somebody else (or other people) and you were not sure what to do.
What did you do?

From the wealth of material obtained from asking these questions, the team were able to gain some insight into the processes of moral and social learning of young people.

These processes are described in McPhail, Middleton, and Ingram (1978), especially chapter 1, where an account is given of the significance of: (a) teachers treating the children considerately if they are to learn to be considerate; (b) social conditioning; (c) sensitivities to verbal and non-verbal communication; (d) imitation of someone respected; (e) trial and error especially in adolescence, 'the age of social experiment'; (f) adjustment through play to novel situations. On the basis of this analysis they were able, too, to draw some conclusions about the kind of school organisation that facilitates moral growth, as the project saw it, 'the practice of doing good things, of actually taking another's needs, feelings and interests into consideration as well as one's own' (McPhail et al., 1978, page 5). The school should be so organised that care is constantly shown for 'the patterns of relationships and encounters within the school', that opportunities are provided 'for children to endeavour to behave responsibly and show initiative', and that contacts with parents and the local community are established which enable 'consistency and continuity in the child's moral development'.

Reference to processes and school organisation is essential if the value of the project's curriculum materials is to be seen in proper perspective. There are three lots of materials: *Photoplay*, *Choosing*, and *Growing*. The 'photoplay materials' focus on moods such as unhappiness or anger; they aim to heighten a child's perceptions of others' needs and feelings and to develop interpersonal skills, especially in communication. The 'choosing materials' provide stories, arising out of the survey of incidents reported as significant by the children, and are used for helping them to make decisions, to deal with others, to deliberate about the consequences and alternatives. The 'growing materials' are essentially a resource bank of situations, arising out of the children's answers to the questions posed above, which require understanding and interpretation within the context of their own social and moral experience.

A detailed account is given in McPhail et al. (1978). But this project is not, I believe, one which is intended to be followed slavishly as though it has the answer to moral growth in young people. Rather does it set an example of the kind of enquiry into young children's feelings and attitudes, as a basis for curriculum development, which classroom teachers could profitably repeat as the starting point for their social education programme.

(vi) Social Awareness in the Early Years (Five and Six)

Many of the examples I have given are taken from the secondary period of schooling. But the theoretical work has stressed the importance of the early years, even though, because of the particular stage of development, the behaviour of the children might not be distinctively moral. One interesting example of a curriculum approach to those early years is described by Olwen Goodall (1983), research officer on a project at Exeter University School of Education, directed by Dr David Evans. The approach used to promote social awareness (a pre-requisite of subsequent moral behaviour, as I have described it in this book) was that developed by Spivack and Shure (1974) with the emphasis on 'the development of personal and interpersonal problem-solving skills that children can incorporate and use when confronted with a variety of typical problem situations'.

The curriculum objectives of the Spivack and Shure interpersonal cognitive problem solving programme were:

Internal-emotional	Cognitive	Overt-behavioural
	Understanding social causation	Developing better interpersonal relations
Accepting self-responsibility	Generating alternative consequences	Increasing communication skills
	Developing self-knowledge	Increasing interpersonal effectiveness
	Gaining ability to talk about emotions	Decreasing discipline problems

To quote Goodall (1983, page 73):

All teaching was based on games and stories, starting initially with teaching the language necessary for social problem-solving, then dealing with recognising different emotions in themselves and others. Consequential thinking is introduced next, and the idea of judging whether a given idea is a good one or a bad one, together with the notion of fairness. The final part of the programme deals with learning to think of many solutions to social problems (how to get to play with a toy that someone else is playing with), and the consequences of solutions.

In Goodall's work there was also an interesting use of brainstorming techniques and of real examples from children's lives. A further interesting feature of this work with very young children is the stress upon learning the language necessary for social problem solving – part of 'understanding social causation'. We have seen in chapters 2 and 3 how this capacity to understand and to relate to others in a meaningful and interpersonal way is integral to personal growth.

One of the several measures which were used to investigate change before and after the programme examined the children's value-system with respect to social justice, using Damon's (1977) systematic description of children's knowledge of fair distribution and sharing. For, although the programme teaches children to generate solutions to problems, these solutions have to be evaluated as good or bad ideas, and the value-system of the children has initially to provide the framework within which such a judgment is made.

The results at this early stage indicate an interesting change in the children's thinking – the conceptual basis on which they decide how to share things out, an awareness of the needs and feelings of others, problem-solving reasoning – although this is not as yet reflected in any obvious way in classroom behaviour.

The next stage of the project has been to get the class teachers more involved so that the approach can be incorporated into normal class contact rather than separated into a special experimental period.[9]

(vii)   Steps to Success

Interpersonal problem-solving is not to be equated with behaving morally, but it is an important part of it – decision making, thinking through the consequences, appealing to principles, especially of fairness, coming to terms with one's own and with others' feelings.

Thacker (1983) describes various programmes aimed at helping young people, many of whom had been described as maladjusted and emotionally disturbed, to improve their ability to solve problems, especially interpersonal ones. The premise from which this work begins is captured in the comment by D'Zurilla and

Goldfried (1971) that much of what is labelled 'emotional disturbance' is ineffective behaviour and its consequences, 'in which the individual is unable to resolve certain situational problems in his life and his inadequate attempts to do so are having undesirable effects, such as anxiety, depression and the creation of additonal problems'.

The stages of a problem solving approach are summarised by Thacker as follows:

(1) General orientation
(2) Problem definition and formulation
(3) Generation of alternatives
(4) Decision making
(5) Verification.

For details of such an approach one must read Thacker, and in particular his teacher's manual with accompanying materials (see Thacker, 1982).

These few examples serve simply to demonstrate two things: first, that there are already attempts to translate theoretical accounts of moral development into curriculum terms, which can be used by teachers in their own practical thinking and planning; secondly, that despite the differences there is a regular emphasis upon (a) certain kinds of thinking skills; (b) the development through various activities of the ability to see things from another person's point of view; (c) an understanding of interpersonal relations and the ability to handle these sensitively; and (d) the significance of school and classroom atmosphere and of trusting, caring relationships between teachers and pupil.

7 Curriculum Consequences

Covering so much territory in one small chapter is clearly inadequate. Especially in the last section some practical projects have been described and their limitations pointed out. Each, however, is worthy of much more detailed examination.

None the less certain general conclusions might be reached that have practical significance:

(i) that there is now a considerable research and curriculum development basis for deciding how one might promote personal, social and moral education;[10]

(ii)   that, none the less, one can analyse specific components (attitudes, reasoning capacities, rules of behaviour, concepts, feelings) that constitute this development and promote these as curriculum objectives;

(iii)   that meanwhile the whole enterprise is shot through with unavoidable problems about the values and 'the sort of person' one is promoting (what sort of autonomy, for example, one has in mind);

(iv)   that early in life there is a need to teach a consistent and defensible set of rules of behaviour, many of which will need to be assimilated as habits;

(v)   that as the child grows older he will need to be encouraged to see the principles that lie behind these rules – and the teacher will need to adopt a much less authoritarian stance in relation to what is right or wrong;

(vi)   that the teacher will need to adopt a very supportive role in helping young people, 'at the age of social experiment', to cope systematically and fairly with their interpersonal problems;

(vii)   that the whole work of the school will need to enhance the sense of personal worth and dignity of each person;

(viii)   that concern for developing the different morally relevant capacities and feelings will need to permeate the general atmosphere and relationships within the school (it is no good preaching fairness and not practising it).

Two major tasks therefore confront the school that intends to take seriously personal, social and moral education. First, there are general questions that should be asked about the curriculum and the life of the school as a whole. Do the school and the curriculum, for instance,

(1)   respect the pupils as persons in the sense of:
    (a)   making allowances for individual differences in feelings and opinions and in the qualitatively different capacities to think their ways through personal and social problems?
    (b)   enbabling them to contribute to that part of school life which affects them personally and morally?

(2)   assist pupils to see others (for example, ethnic minorities) as persons in the sense described?

(3)   enable pupils to see themselves as persons in this sense and, as such, worthy of self-respect and of the respect of others?

(4) encourage that independence of thought, that systematic reflective thinking, which is summed up by the word autonomy?

These more general questions we shall examine in the next chapter – the impact, if you like, of the hidden curriculum.

Secondly, apart from thinking about the impact of the curriculum and the life of the school as a whole, the school needs to consider how and where there needs to be specific teaching to ensure that the different aspects of personal, social, and moral education, as analysed, can be acquired. I have given a few examples of such teaching, but this will require some more detailed mapping out of the curriculum territory which will be attempted in chapter 6.

NOTES

1 This philosophical position was clearly expounded by Ayer (1946). The central feature of logical positivism, as it was called, was its 'principle of verification'. The principle of verification, as he outlined it, provided a criterion of meaning; a statement is literally meaningful if and only if it is true analytically or can be verified. He explained that a statement is verifiable if you know what kind of observations would enable you to decide, under certain conditions, whether or not the statement was true. One can see how moral, religious, aesthetic, and political statements fared under this criterion of meaning. It is not clear (so it is argued) that observations will enable statements within these areas to be verified. Hence, they are rejected as pseudo-statements. For criticisms of logical positivism, and in particular the emotive theory of ethics, one should read Warnock (1966).

2 Two major books by Hare are *The Language of Morals* (1952) and *Freedom and Reason* (1963). His argument is developed, and critics are answered, in a recent book *Moral Thinking* (1981). What makes a particular prescription moral is its form rather than its content, and one needs to learn these formal properties – or at least learn how to apply them consistently and logically. Again one might turn to Warnock (1966) for a critical appraisal of 'prescriptivism' as this philosophical position is referred to.

3 Current perspectives on the theory and practice of behaviour modification are given in the University of Exeter's *Perspectives 5*. There I argue that the theory has value within very strict limits which its proponents often fail to recognise (see Pring, 1981).

4   The philosophical position referred to here is sometimes called 'intuitionism'. Whereas some philosophers have argued that there are no moral facts and that moral statements are not proper statements at all (they either *express* feeling or *prescribe* a course of action; see pages 57, 58, and notes 1 and 2 above), intuitionists assert that there are moral facts, and that there *are* moral statements which are true or false in so far as they correspond with the moral facts. It is argued that there is a limit to how far one can go back in justifying as morally right what one believes, and so ultimately one reaches a set of moral claims which require no further justification. They are the ultimate moral truths which one just *sees* to be true. Perhaps, of course, on this view some people have better insight than others – others are 'morally blind'. For that reason Plato argues in *The Republic* for special training for political leaders who will thereby gain access to the 'good' on behalf of everyone and who will be able therefore to guide others who have not got that insight (see Plato's *The Republic*, Penguin 1955 edition; also Warnock's 1966 criticism of intuitionism).

5   The many different shades of meaning, of both philosophical and educational interest, are described by Ward (1983).

6   Fenton and Kohlberg's *Teacher Training in Values Education: A Workshop* was published by Guidance Associates in 1976. It is a self-instructional kit that presents a basic introduction to Kohlberg's work and its implications for the classroom. The kit includes four sound filmstrips, a series of worksheets on duplicating masters for use by teachers or workshop participants, and plans for using this material – in the classroom or in a workshop. Guidance Associates published other kits, too, that introduce and apply the theoretical framework of Kohlberg: (a) Fenton and Kohlberg (1976b) *Universal Values in American History*, which consists of twenty moral dilemmas designed for use in junior and senior high school American history courses (with accompanying sound filmstrips, duplicating masters, theoretical rationale, and suggested lesson plans); and (b) Fenton and Kohlberg (1976c) *Values in a Democracy* which contains twenty moral dilemmas designed for use in civics or 'problems of democracy' courses. Mosher (1980) has provided us with lots of examples of 'a first generation of research and development' in moral education in which the theoretical perspective of Kohlberg is translated into practice. Scharf (1978) gives a lucid account of Kohlberg's developmental theory together with examples of its application to the classroom.

7   The Farmington Trust was established in 1965 to conduct research on the topic of moral education. John Wilson was its first director and initially there were two research fellows, Norman Williams, a psychologist, and Barry Sugarman, a sociologist. Their joint publication *Introduction to Moral Education* in 1967 was the first publication of the Trust and a valuable illustration of an interdisciplinary

approach to moral education. Books by Wilson on ethics and moral education are: *Reason and Morals* (1961), which anticipated many of the ideas of the *Introduction to Moral Education; Moral Education and the Curriculum* (1969), which, following the theoretical framework established in the *Introduction*, offered 'a guide for research on the topic, which teachers and others are invited to use in conjunction with their own experience and reflections'; and *A Teacher's Guide to Moral Education* (1973) which translated the theoretical framework into more practical curriculum terms. The thinking of the Trust about the social context of moral education – the influence of the school as an institution upon moral development – was contained in Sugarman's *The School and Moral Development* (1973).

8   Papers and publications relevant to the Schools Council moral education projects are these:

   (i)   *Moral Education 13 to 16* (Lifeline)
         Teachers' books: *Moral Education in the Secondary School* by McPhail, Ungoed-Thomas and Chapman, (1972), which looks at the theory and practice of moral education, describes its study of pupils' needs, and introduces the Lifeline materials. *Our School* by Ungoed-Thomas (1972) which is a handbook on the practice of democracy in schools.
         Pupils' materials: *In Other People's Shoes*, which consists of three sets of cards ('Points of View', 'Consequences', and 'Sensitivity') presenting situations as starting points for pupils' consideration of consequences and others' points of view and circumstances; *Proving the Rule*, which consists of five illustrated books containing brief accounts of the relationships of a young man with his family, friends, society; *What would you have done?* which consists of six booklets considering moral and social problems in a worldwide context. All materials are published by Longman under the title *Lifeline*.
   (ii) *Moral Education 8 to 13* (Startline)
         Teachers' books: *Startline: Moral Education in the Middle Years* by McPhail, Middleton, and Ingram (1978) which, based on a survey of children, describes the processes of social and moral learning and the curriculum materials developed to promote it. *The Moral Situation of Children* by Ungoed-Thomas (1978) which describes in detail the research into how young children think and feel about moral and social situations.
         Pupils' (or Startline) materials: *Choosing* which is a series of six short collections of children's own personal experiences. These help the pupils to identify how and where they can affect their own course of action, partly through identifying and evaluating alternative courses of action; *Photoplay 1 and 2*, relevant posters and cards; *Growing*, which presents situations

where children were happy or unhappy and which encourage them to develop understanding of themselves and of others in a considerate way. All the materials are published by Longman under the title *Startline*.

9   A workbook arising out of the workshops and out of experience with a group of teachers is about to be published. It will be available upon request from University of Exeter School of Education. See Goodall *et al.* (1983). The workshops, supported by both the Devon local education authority and the University of Exeter, were intended as a pilot scheme which could become the basis of work elsewhere, especially at teachers' centres. The workshops looked at certain theoretical ideas (including the research that Goodall had conducted over a three year period) which had implications for the social behaviour, attitudes, and personal experience of young children (five- to eight-year-olds). The key question was how might these ideas be translated into classroom practice. The workbook is essentially a guide: to classroom practice, to action research into practice, and to analysis of the teacher's own attitudes that affect practice. There are quite a few examples of what teachers might try out and there are useful lists of resources.

10 The following books not explicitly mentioned in the text, are valuable general contributions to our understanding of moral education: Peters (1974b) *Psychology and Ethical Development*, which is a collection of articles on psychological theories, ethical development, and human understanding; Wright (1971) *The Psychology of Moral Behaviour*; Bull (1969), *Moral Education*; Kay (1970), *Moral Development: a psychological study of moral growth from childhood to adolescence*; Kay (1975), *Moral Education: a sociological study of the influence of society, home and school*; Straughan (1982), *Can We Teach Children to be Good?*; and McPhail (1982), *Social and Moral Education*.

PART II

Curriculum

5 Curriculum Context

1 Introduction

There is no doubt in many people's minds that personal, social, and moral development should be a major concern of the schools. But it is mistaken to conclude that the way of translating this concern into curriculum terms is to put another subject, namely, personal and social education, into the timetable. It *might* be important to look at the content of the curriculum – that we shall consider in the next chapter – but the upshot of what I have argued so far is that there are more significant questions to be asked about the conditions of learning, the impact of the curriculum as a whole upon the young person, the methods of teaching and the relationships between teacher and pupil. Indeed, to add yet another subject to the already overcrowded timetable could be seen as a way of escaping from these questions.

Let us consider this general point in greater detail whilst referring back to the tentative conclusions already reached. Young persons, as they grow older, are learning far more from the behaviour and attitudes of those around them than they are from formal instruction. Indeed, a clear message coming from the adolescents interviewed by McPhail *et al.* (1972) was that instruction in how to behave had little impact where it was not reflected in the attitudes and behaviour of the instructors.

Or, again, at the centre of any personal development (and indirectly of moral development) is the respect young persons must achieve for themselves as persons, but that requires a sense of their own value to others and of competence in the tasks they handle. No amount of instruction in personal, social, and moral development can compensate for the destruction of dignity that the constant experience of failure brings to so many pupils. But to provide this sense of personal worth and competence requires not another subject but a way of approaching old subjects and of relating to young persons.

Or, again, respect for other people and an appreciation of how they think or feel are key elements in what I have been saying, but the growth of respect and appreciation require, not a subject called 'empathy', but the insights that can be afforded through literature, history, and so on, if these are taught in a particular way.

Or, again, we have seen from Piaget and the other developmental theorists how personal growth goes step in step with a changing relationship to authority – from one of unilateral respect to one of mutual respect. Too authoritarian an approach to rules, to discipline, to relationships between teacher and pupil, or to the subject matter of the curriculum itself, will encourage a spirit of dependence, an immaturity of outlook, and a failure to reach the kind of autonomy in which a young person can take responsibility for his or her own life.

Or, again, we saw in relation to Kohlberg the importance of properly conducted discussions in the development of a person's competence in handling social and moral issues – a shift from didactic to reflective learning, and from teacher dependence to acceptance of responsibility for decisions reached.

Above all, however, there is the stress throughout the research upon the social context in which development takes place. Get that social context wrong and development will be stunted. For Piaget, the development of intelligence was not a condition for co-operation; rather was co-operative behaviour a condition for the growth of intelligence.

One can see, therefore, the resistance to personal and social development, whatever the lip service paid to it by placing it, as a subject, on the curriculum. First, we are unfortunately so concerned with rewarding the few and with distributing talent along a 'normal curve of distribution', that we often cannot imagine an educational system that does not produce failures in the same proportion as it produces successes. Far from encouraging sharing and co-operation, we make learning from the start a competitive and individual exercise. Secondly, so often educational administrators, university lecturers, head teachers and classroom teachers hide behind a facade of authority that requires 'unilateral respect', rather than the 'mutual respect' I have (following Piaget) been talking about. At eleven years of age, my eldest daughter attended sixth grade of an American elementary school. What struck her most forcibly was the increased maturity of her classmates in comparison with their English counterparts. Bussed into a down-town school in a predominantly black area with a lot of social (including unemployment) problems, she was surprised at the lack of silliness in the classroom, the mature way in which personal conflicts were resolved, the unselfconscious relationships be-tween boys and girls, the indifference to the quality and fashion of what other pupils were wearing. Quizzed about the possible causes of this, she put it down to a different classroom atmosphere in which relationships between teacher and pupil were (in her words) more equal. 'They talk to you and explain things to you, as though you are a grown up.' Well, treat others in a spirit of mutual respect and no doubt you will be treated likewise.

One day my six-year-old in grade two was near to tears because she had been teased – she was new to the school, was English, and had two new stitches in a gashed eyebrow, and was therefore (according to the logic of six-year-olds) a suitable target for teasing. The class teacher took considerable trouble to find the boy (in another class), not to tell him off or to punish him or to force him to apologise, but to explain how his teasing had hurt someone and how this was not the way in which the school could become a friendly and pleasant place. I was in the school at the time and was embarrassed at the trouble taken. But to the teacher this was the normal way of handling this kind of problem – such social and moral learning was more important than the academic. No need to wonder, therefore, at the more considerate, mature behaviour by the time children reached the top of the elementary school.

Doubtless readers will be able to recall many instances where questionable behaviour of pupils became not an interference with the curriculum but a focus of the curriculum itself – an opportu-nity, within the right school and classroom atmosphere, to foster the personal and social growth of the class as a whole. Indeed, this would feature as a regular part of the personal and social education curricula that are being developed in many schools, especially for the pupils of low achievement. But success in this requires a particular kind of relationship between teacher and pupil, and a particular approach to learning. Let me illustrate this by one incident at a local high school. A group of fourth year non-examination pupils were, as part of their alternative social studies curriculum, working in a primary school with five-year-old chil-dren. The fourteen-year-olds had one thing in common, namely, their low achievement in academic subjects, but there were sev-eral, too, with behavioural problems. They were teaching the five-year-olds to use money. Subsequently it was discovered that some money was missing.

There were two possible ways of handling the situation. The first was to engage the normal disciplinary procedure of the school to detect the thieves and to hand out punishment. The second was to place the problem in the hands of the group – a risky business since the group itself was not noted for its sense of responsibility. Given this responsibility, however, a morning was spent discussing the incident, realising the consequences, detecting which of their number were responsible, and deliberating what should be done. Finally it was decided *by the group* that the culprits should personally take the missing money back to the primary school headmaster and apologise to the five-year-olds.

This incident is worth analysing closely. First, the theft was not treated as an unfortunate distraction from a preplanned programme of social education – it became 'the curriculum'. Secondly, it required a relationship of 'mutual respect' (see page 38) between teacher and pupil in which the pupils could trust the teacher to keep confidences and in which the teacher could place trust in the deliberations of the group. Thirdly, the success of the deliberations depended partly on being away from the ethos of 'unilateral respect' that prevails in most institutions, especially schools; they took place in a local youth club. Fourthly, the teacher managed to harness the powerful force of peer approval/disapproval rather than use her own authority in motivating the culprits to see the significance of what had been done. If Kohlberg is correct, it is doubtful whether these young people would have been moved by appeal to abstract principles of fairness or to social obligations, but they could begin to see the force of values which in fact were related to general well-being and which were upheld by the group they identified with.

The context, however, in which the appropriate relationships and modes of social learning are established, can be examined at different levels. The school and especially the teachers within that school are severely restricted in how far they can change the context in which they have to carry out their task. These 'levels', then, we shall examine in greater detail.

2 School and Society

There are several ways in which the school incorporates and transmits wider social values. Sometimes these are quite overt. For example, secondary schools have been criticised in recent years for not preparing young people adequately for the world of work. This purported lack of preparation lies in three areas: an unfavourable attitude towards 'wealth-producing' industries upon which social welfare indirectly depends; an ignorance of business, commerce, and industry; and a lack of those basic skills which efficient employment will depend upon. In consequence, efforts are being made to help schools become more vocationally oriented: for example, the ideas and practices embodied in the pre-vocational courses of further education colleges (see FEU, 1979) are increasingly being incorporated into the work of the schools; the Schools Council School and Industry Project has been widely disseminated and taken up with alacrity by schools;[1] and the *14 to 18* initiatives of the Manpower Services Commission for pilot schemes of technical and vocational education provoked prompt replies from over seventy local education authorities.[2] This stress upon economic and social utility is having its effect – it is competing (successfully in some quarters of education) with a more liberal and humanistic tradition in which the value of social and economic utility is subordinate to that of cultivating the powers of the mind. The point here is that wider social values begin to enter the curriculum, thereby affecting the values that are transmitted to young people, as a result of explicit social and educational policy. Those who are concerned with personal and social education will need to attend critically to these quite explicit values which can permeate the curriculum as a whole. There are of course ways in which society's values enter the life of the school (thereby affecting the personal growth of individual pupils) through legislation. The 1975 Sex Discrimination Act ensures that there will be no discrimination between boys and girls in the provision of educational resources or curriculum openings. There has been ample evidence of the many ways in which, through schooling, girls learn to be 'certain sorts of person' – submissive, unambitious, accepting a particular role in life, setting sights lower than those of boys, non-scientific, and so on. No legislation will eradicate the subtle ways in which – through teachers' attitudes and curriculum content – these 'messages' are conveyed. But it can be an important element in changing attitudes. Girls now learn that they, too, can achieve success at traditionally boys' activities – metalwork, woodwork, technical drawing, physics, mathematics. Teachers become increasingly sensitive to accusations of sex bias. This is, of course, an extensive area of investigation and it is not possible to go into detail here. What is important for my purposes is to signal the importance for personal development (especially development into 'a particular sort of person', as I defined this in chapter 2) of the ways in which sex stereotyping and sex role differentiation takes place through the life of the school and can be affected by positive Government policy as this is reflected in legislation.[3]

It would be mistaken, however, to confine one's attention to explicit values, for more important are the hidden values reflected in the educational system. A lot has been written recently about the way in which the school reflects the values of society and, quite unknowingly, socialises pupils into ways of seeing, appreciating, and experiencing the world, in particular the social world of power, authority, status, and relationships. On the one hand, there are the Marxist critiques such as that of Bowles and Gintis (1976), according to which schools simply reflect and reproduce the values of a capitalist society. Within such a determinist account of schooling, the efforts of the individual or school are fruitless; we may think, as teachers, that we are forming autonomous, critical future citizens, but in fact we are simply reinforcing a class structure, with different individuals being allocated to different roles within such a society.

There are, however, several accounts of how ideology (the dominant framework of ideas that permeate how we value, interpret, and explain things) enters into our everyday lives, especially in the day to day practices of school. Apple (1979), for example, is critical of the large-scale deterministic analysis of Bowles and Gintis but shows how none the less the structural features of our society do enter into the relationships and the values being promoted in the classroom. According to Apple, the classroom should be seen as a place where different 'meanings' are contested (how the teacher understands social reality as against how the pupils, especially those from different social classes, understand it) and where these different meanings are negotiated, frequently to the advantage of the teacher who is the dominant partner in the 'negotiation'.

This is not the place to examine in detail such critiques, but it is important to see the relevance at the common-sense level of the points these writers are making. The wider social and political order does demand a hierarchical differentiation of roles. There are different levels of bosses in most big factories, and the work-force is not always encouraged to participate, in a real and responsible way, in the policy-making of the factory or in the distribution of rewards. An essential condition therefore for maintaining such social differentiation is the creation of an ordered and obedient society with clear lines of authority and with fairly compliant workers. One can see how the conditions for such social stratification are implicitly supported by certain forms of schooling – with an insistence upon authority, a discouragement of critical questioning, an habituation to a place in society without responsibilities and a dependence upon others to make decisions. I know of a school that makes pupils prefects at the age of eleven. The majority of pupils of course do not get chosen; they are learning fairly early what their position in society is going to be. Uniform is *de rigueur* even to the length of trousers – above the knee before the age of eleven whatever one's shape or size. Being regulated down to the minutest detail of one's life is something these children will, after seven years of schooling, have come to accept as 'natural'.

It is of course paradoxical that these values and attitudes, which the school system is claimed to promote, should be appropriate for an industrial scene that is quickly passing. The large factories, requiring a relatively submissive work-force that can be trusted to carry out routine tasks, are in decline. Hope for the future lies to a greater extent than hitherto in the small enterprise, employing relatively few people who will participate more closely in deliberations about the quality and efficiency of the work and who will be expected to take on a variety of tasks. Greater responsibility amongst the employees, and more initiative and entrepreneurial skills amongst an increasing number of small employers, could be the scene of the future. Commenting on the American situation Feldman (1981) argues for the increasing importance of the small business and criticises the American high school for still preparing young people for the obsolescent large organisation in which the spirit of creativity and entrepreneurship is irrelevant to the large majority of workers.[4]

The relation of school to society was of course at the centre of Dewey's thinking. An emerging society, that needed to integrate a large immigrant population from many different cultures, saw a particular type of education (controlled and conducted democratically and encouraging as wide a social continuum of experience as possible) to be an essential condition of success. In *Democracy and Education*, Dewey (1916) spelt out the educational philosophy required for the sort of society he, inheriting the democratic tradition of America, thought desirable. But the relation of one to the other was not one of cause to effect. The school had to embody, in its very relationships and teaching methods and exercise of authority, the values that, in theory at least, typified the new state of America. If you want a just society you need to create just individuals. But if you want to create just individuals, you need to create just institutions and relationships within which they can learn justice. This aspect of Dewey's philosophy was taken up by Kohlberg as we shall see in the next section.

The following examples are intended to illustrate these general points. The first two are closely related, as I shall point out, but this is rarely recognised.

First, my eldest daughter has recently gone to the local high school (which in Exeter is the local comprehensive where a four-tier system is operated). Some of her friends, however, will be saying goodbye in order to go to one of three private girls' schools where they will learn that they are different from the likes of her and the others at the comprehensive. Such a movement of middle-class children is being encouraged both openly by the present Government in its policy of privatisation of education (see Pring, 1983) and covertly through the very large subsidies given to these relatively privileged children. The process is quite frightening. My children's education is being conducted by teachers, guided by governors, administered by officers, and controlled by politicians, who, however, send their own children to private school. It is as though they are saying that the work they are responsible for is only of second-class value, but none the less good enough for other people's children. This, to me, quite disgraceful state of affairs constitutes a most significant part of the differentiated social learning of young people which is quite ignored by many who otherwise are so keen on personal and social education. Of course, in coming to understand this parting of the ways, my daughter has learnt about and come to appreciate certain social values and conditions, an important part, I hope, of her personal growth.

The point of this example is that wider social policies (not only permitting but actively encouraging a private sector) enter into the values of schooling and of teaching, and into how individual youngsters perceive their status in society and their relationships with others.

The second example is from curriculum developments taking place in the 14 to 18 age range. Increasingly, the more vocationally oriented approach to learning, which characterises the pre-vocational programmes of further education, is entering schools, and this has been embodied in the technical and vocational education initiatives (TVEI, see note 2, page 111) of the Manpower Services Commission. Such a curriculum is characterised by vocational relevance, experiential learning, technological studies, skills acquisition, social (including political) understanding, social and life skills, communications, and numeracy. These developments *could* be quite exciting if interpreted generously (see Brockington, White and Pring, 1983, and FEU, 1984) but it is doubtful whether they will be: witness the absence of any reference, for example, to the expressive arts. Thus 'social and life skills' could become the learning of a limited range of behaviours for coping with a particular kind of social role; 'social and political education' could become the knowledge about certain social and political institutions; 'communication' could become the skills of form-filling and letter writing; 'experiential learning' could become work experience in fairly repetitive jobs. Far from being exciting, this could lead to a culturally limited curriculum for a majority of pupils – a return of the elementary tradition (stressing the practical, the useful, and the skilful) to the maintained schools whilst increasingly those who know where real power lies will escape to the subsidised private sector where the ideals of a liberal and non-vocational education are valued.

Thirdly, it is difficult to see how any programme of personal and social education can ignore either the political values or the political skills required for participating in those activities and choices which affect one's own welfare. We are seeing, however, how sensitive different authorities are becoming to those schools who take this part of personal and social education seriously. Youth training schemes which, as part of social education, were helping young people to analyse what was of personal concern to them (namely, unemployment or poor job prospects) were told to drop controversial topics or else they would not be funded. One education authority banned from its schools political education after a student-teacher was reported to have recited in class Peter Porter's poem 'Seven Ways to Die'. The ban was withdrawn before the meeting of full council. Later, however, the teaching of peace studies was forbidden because of its political significance. (Meanwhile, war games are played, unaffected, as part of some schools' curricula.) The APU exploratory group on personal and social development were referred to in the press as a bunch of Nazis because they were considering the possibility of monitoring this area of the curriculum.

The point of these last incidents is this. What happens in school, particularly in the area of personal and social education, will inevitably have some political significance. That is, it will affect how children think about and relate to those who, at national and local levels, exercise power and influence over them. And this in turn is likely to affect how the custodians of social values will relate to the school and to what the school is doing. Encouraging children to think about issues of war and peace might well be considered dangerous if the children have thoughts which are not acceptable to the party in power. This problem is quickly emerging over the teaching of peace studies. And yet is not the banning of discussion on nuclear arms policy (unless based upon the information sheets coming out of the Central Office of Information) an excellent example of Benjamin's (1971) 'Sabre tooth curriculum'?

To return to the theoretical perspective in Part I (and harking back to what HMI said in *Curriculum 11 to 16* which I quoted on page 5), the problem might be stated in these terms. With the increasing interdependence of different social, ethnic and national groups, there is a need for people to think more readily at Kohlberg's post-conventional level, answering practical, moral problems by appeal to principles that transcend specific social or cultural boundaries. That partly is what the autonomous and educated person should be capable of. On the other hand, the preservation of national self-interest as it comes to be defined at any one time requires not too many people who can 'universalise their principles'. The level of conventional morality might be all that the politician can tolerate.

3   School Ethos and Classroom Atmosphere

Rutter *et al.* (1979) was an interesting study of twelve different schools in the Inner London Education Authority. The main question it raised was: do schools make a difference? To answer this question the study needed to identify certain outcomes which would seem to be significant indicators of the differences that schools make – examination results, pupil behaviour and pupil attendance. Furthermore, it tried to analyse those factors which were most closely correlated with these differences in outcomes. Such a report has inevitably been subjected to extensive criticism, and indeed it has been most careful not to confuse correlations with causes and effects. None the less, the results are quite startling. Schools that seemed roughly comparable in social and physical conditions produced very different results. Poor behaviour, for example, measured in terms of vandalism, graffiti, bullying, rudeness and so on, was significantly different in different schools, where these differences could not be accounted for in terms of the values or behaviours or expectations that the pupils brought with them into the schools. The report correlated these outcomes not with any single factors but with clusters of factors. What above all seemed significant was the 'ethos' of the school.

This is a vague and difficult term, but Dancy (1980) does, in the light of Rutter, analyse it in terms of the values, aims, attitudes, and procedures of a school which interrelate and which remain a relatively permanent feature of the school. For example, one can identify certain regular procedures in the life of the school, such as displaying the work of pupils, which reflect attitudes towards pupils and towards work, which in turn are reflected in the school's aims (even if these are not made explicit) and ultimately the dominant values of the school. To get at the ethos of the school, you need to examine the various stable procedures through which business is conducted towards the individual and his or her work, towards the community as a whole, and towards those outside the school. And picking out these significant procedures is exactly what Rutter did. What correlated highly with approved behaviour were such procedures as displaying children's work on the wall, recognising achievement through praise, preparing thoroughly for lessons, displaying as often as possible trust in pupils by giving them responsible tasks, turning up punctually for class. The account given on pages 182–98 of Rutter (1979) could be used by a school as a basis for examining its own particular 'ethos'.

A slightly different point is made by Hargreaves (1982) when he writes about the hidden curriculum of the school. This is the values, connected with general ethos maybe, which are transmitted to pupils through the kinds of relationships and practices which prevail within the school. They are hidden because they are not acknowledged in the formal curriculum, but they may have a more lasting effect. In fact, it is Hargreave's argument (on page 17) that

> . . . our present secondary school system, largely through the hidden curriculum, exerts on many pupils, particularly but by no means exclusively from the working class, a destruction of their dignity which is so massive and pervasive that few subsequently recover from it.

Hargreaves' is a devastating attack upon the pretensions of schools who claim to be fostering personal and social development, where the sense of personal worth is near destroyed through the constant experience of failure and through the lack of respect felt for those values which they, the pupils, prize most dearly and which they bring with them into the school. I say 'near destroyed' because Hargreaves points to the various ways in which youngsters preserve a sense of dignity, often finding refuge in a shared opposition to what the school offers or in a rebellion against authority, or in an assertion of *their* different cultural values (in their style, dress, language, music, and so on) – the social world described so aptly by Willis (1977).

In some respects this is not a new 'discovery'. Philip Jackson's (1968) *Life in Classrooms* and John Holt (1964) in *How Children Fail* pointed to the strategies that children adopt to disguise failure and to survive with dignity in classrooms. But Hargreaves probes more deeply into the underlying values – the cult of individualism, the importance attached to academic achievement to the exclusion of personal and social values, the narrow interpretation of success, the limited view of 'worthwhile culture', the diminishing significance attached to the expressive arts and to emotional response. In Hargreaves there is a link between the educational values of the school (as they are embedded but rarely made explicit in the formal curriculum) and the perception of his or her worth by each pupil, which reinforces the significance of the question posed on page 31 of this book: 'What is the impact of the curriculum as a whole upon the sense of personal worth experienced by each pupil?'

Hargreaves' solution in general terms is that we need to think much more of the school as a community rather than as an aggregate of individuals and of how the sense of solidarity might be fostered. The battle for comprehensive education has for long been fought in terms of individual freedom versus equality of opportunity. The third element of fraternity has, until Hargreaves resurrected it, been largely neglected since Dewey (1916) and perhaps Tawney (1938). To quote Tawney in his corrective to the exaggerated emphasis upon individual advancement which we see in education:

> . . . in spite of their varying character and capacities, men possess in their common humanity a quality which is worth cultivating and . . . a community is most likely to make the most of that quality if it takes it into account in planning its economic organisation and social institutions – if it stresses lightly differences of wealth and birth and social position, and establishes on firm foundations institutions which meet common needs, and are a source of common enlightenment and common enjoyment.
>
> (pages 55–6)

Hence by way of solution, Tawney suggests (page 17) that, in addition to getting rid of gross inequalities of wealth:

> What a community requires, as the word itself suggests, is a common culture, because, without it, it is not a community at all.

The connection between a sense of community (or of social solidarity) and personal dignity is two-fold. First, the sense of solidarity with others does itself engender a recognition of their humanity – that they are like oneself in having feelings, aspirations, ambitions, and so on. Secondly, however, the respect given to individuals reflects the respect given to the groups to which they belong – and thus the respect given to the institutions which particular groups attend. There is a touch of hypocrisy in the current concern for personal development where the institutional context is ignored – where, for example, the disintegrating force of private education is being actively promoted and where, within the maintained sector, divisions between types of school and types of curriculum are being created.

How do these points relate to the theoretical perspectives developed earlier in this book? According to Piaget (1932, page 134):

> Young people need to find themselves in the presence not of a system of commands requiring ritualistic and external obedi-

ence, but a system of social relations such that everyone does his best to obey the same obligations, and does so out of mutual respect.

The qualitative improvement in judgment mapped out by both Piaget and Kohlberg required the right social conditions. And indeed it was this, anticipated in Dewey's democratically run community school, that Kohlberg (1982, page 24) tried to capture in his 'Just Community' Schools.

> In summary, the current demand for moral education is a demand that our society becomes more of a just community. If our society is to become a more just community, it needs democratic schools. This was the demand and dream of Dewey.

The experiment with a 'Just Community' approach to education is described by Wasserman and Garrod (1983, page 17). The hypothesis was

> . . . that by building collective norms and ideas of community at a stage higher than that of many of the members of the group, more responsible student action would be promoted.

This required participatory democracy in which staff and students shared equally in socio-moral decisions about the rules and disciplines of the school. It was hoped thereby that pupils would assume greater responsibility for decisions that affected their welfare and that, in having to think through the problems democratically, they would develop into a more caring community. It was assumed, as Dewey had assumed, that a group of individuals might operate at a higher moral stage of deliberation and judgment than that of the individual members of the group. If that is the case, then, as teachers concerned with the moral development of young people, we should attempt 'to reform the moral atmosphere in which the individual decisions are made'.

In June 1974, the 'Cluster School' was established within the much larger Cambridge High and Latin School, near Boston, Massachusetts, committed to the idea of a 'just community' in which key decisions would be thought through democratically in the light of principled thinking. The enrolment in this 'school within a school' was fifty to seventy students aged fifteen to eighteen. A central part of the formal curriculum was English and social studies which centred on moral discussion, role-taking and communications (see pages 39–46) and on relating the power and authority structure of the school to those of the wider society. Key elements, however, were first, the significance of the issues discussed (significant both to the well-being of the individuals and to the running of the community), and, secondly, responsibility for policy and action shared between staff and pupils. Such discussion and decision-making were at the centre rather than the periphery of the curriculum, and the focus of deliberation in handling these different issues (drug abuse, disruptive behaviour, truanting, distribution of grades, and so on) was upon 'fairness' (see chapter 4, section 6 (ii) of this book).

The main elements in these deliberations might be summarised as follows:

1   *exposure to cognitive moral conflict* over real issues arising within the school community, for example, loyalty to a student who has stolen from another member;
2   *role-taking*, for example, trying to understand things from the thief's point of view;
3   *considerations of fairness and morality*, as seen by the individuals within the group, for example, examining the stealing case in terms of the conventional or legal morality;
4   *exposure to the next higher stage of moral reasoning*, for example, getting those who are at the pre-conventional stage of moral judgment to answer questions concerning the stealing episode, posed in terms of group loyalty and commitment;
5   *active participation in group decision making*, for example, the group deciding both the rules about stealing and the punishment, if any, to be given to the culprit.

How a group came to handle the rules, and their implementation, concerning theft is retold in detail by Wasserman (1976).

It should be emphasised, however, that the success of such an approach depends upon the 'moral atmosphere' of the school; it is no good expecting the students to deliberate and act fairly if the context in which they are doing this is blatantly unfair, or to act out of 'mutual respect' if the expectations of the authorities within the school are of relationships characterised by unilateral respect. Furthermore, considerable skill is required on the part of the staff to stimulate the higher levels of moral discussion and responsible behaviour.

For more details on the conduct of discussions and on the evaluation of this approach, one should read Wasserman and Garrod (1983). Clearly there were risks in the approach, and problems were encountered. But the risks paid off. There was a measurable improvement in the level of moral discussion, a greater concern for the well-being of the community as a whole was shown, and other schools within the school district adopted many of the principles and techniques. These developments are reported in Mosher (1980).

What conclusions might we draw from this, for it may seem much too radical for most English schools (although there are examples of schools which have adopted similar approaches, though not with such a clear theoretical backing; see Watts, 1977, on the Countesthorpe experience)? First, there is the need to ensure that the school *is* a 'moral community' not only because it seriously raises issues of fairness and of concern to the young people but also because it can be seen to act fairly. Secondly, since the issues that concern young people most will be about how they are treated within the school, then the school rules and disciplines and the pupils' perceptions of the school must be treated seriously, and openly discussed as part of the curriculum. (One feature of fairness is that people know how decisions are made and can challenge them in the light of principles to which, in theory, the institution subscribes.) Thirdly, teachers need to acquire the skills of organising discussion and of stimulating deliberation at increasingly higher levels of moral thinking. Finally, greater responsibility must be given to the young people over the action that follows from the deliberations. If that appears a little risky, then perhaps one could start with less significant issues (like school uniform). But too often school councils are a yawn to most pupils because the issues are not about matters of fairness within the school and because the deliberations do not relate directly to action.

4   Thought into Behaviour

In chapter 3, I raised the problem of the link between moral judgment and moral behaviour. Kohlberg has often been criticised for concentrating upon the rational aspect of morality whereas it is how people behave (what they do to each other) that most people are concerned about. However, I pointed out in chapter 4 the misconceptions and dangers of thinking exclusively of behaviour. But the connection between judgment and behaviour had not properly been resolved. In fact certain experiments threw doubt upon the connection: students who had become much more sophisticated in moral discussion continued as before to cheat on experimental tests (see Blatt and Kohlberg, 1975). To some extent this is not surprising; as Power and Reimer (1978) pointed out, there is much more to behaving morally than making the appropriate judgments. An immature person (see my account of Loevinger in chapter 3, pages 47–51) will lack the inner strength to go against the pressure of the group, and even a more developed personality may fail to act on his or her better judgment where pressures are great and where the wrong behaviour does not weigh very greatly *vis-à-vis* other concerns. (Indeed the amount of cheating in experimental tests of moral behaviour could be accounted for by the apparently trivial nature of the activity.) Or, again, one's position and status in society will affect how one sees things; the more status conscious one is the more threatened one might be by taking seriously certain kinds of moral deliberations. (How easy is it for an aspiring conservative politician to take seriously the moral arguments against possessing nuclear weapons, or for the convinced socialist to attend to the moral arguments for the right to private medicine and education?)

None the less, we are now possibly a little nearer to seeing the connection between judgment and action. Too often, possibly under the influential ideal of autonomy, we have thought about the translation of individual judgment into individual action as though the social context were an irrelevant sideshow. But what is emerging from our theoretical account is the central importance of the hidden curriculum or the social context for developing or for stunting personal growth (for example, gaining ego strength in the sense described by Loevinger); or social growth (for example, in relating to authority as described by Piaget or in acquiring an intelligent understanding of the other as described by Selman); or moral growth (for example, in getting beyond the self-interested 'morality' as described by Kohlberg). Therefore, it was concluded by Kohlberg that concern for moral growth must be translated not simply into discussions about morality but into the creation of moral communities. It is important to create the right kind of ethos, the right kind of social atmosphere, in which judgment will be translated into action. Two features of this social atmosphere need to be picked out: the prevailing norms or values within the group and the sense of community for which one learns to care.

Power and Reimer describe their analysis of the moral atmosphere of the school based upon transcripts of community meetings, interviews with individual students about the school, and observations of the interactions between students and teachers in different situations. The five questions they were investigating were:

1 What are the collective normative values operating in the school (for example, trusting implicitly in others' honesty)?
2 How well established and how influential upon individuals are those normative values?
3 What sense of community has developed in the school?
4 How well established and influential upon individuals is the sense of community?
5 At what stage of moral thinking are the students in their perceptions of, and talk about, these normative values and this sense of community?

Power and Reimer noted a developmental sequence in both the normative values within a group and in the sense of community. Furthermore, they noted that as these developed, so the individuals in their judgment and behaviour developed accordingly. The general point is that, contrary to so many attempts to explain moral development (in particular the development of persons within whom there is little or no conflict between higher levels of moral thinking and how they typically behave), the connection between thought and action depends upon the general atmosphere and expectations of the wider community. How individuals behave will so often depend upon the values that are operating in public life and upon the interaction between the individual and those values within a developed sense of community.

5 Conclusion

Personal, social, and moral education requires serious examination of the wider context within which the formal curriculum is planned and taught – whether this be the values that are transmitted from the society outside the school and are embodied within its very structure and system, or whether this be the school or classroom atmosphere (or what Rutter calls 'ethos') within which the teacher is working. At the wider level of social values (for example, the selective function of the school within a stratified society, or the increasingly utilitarian approach to the curriculum) there is a need for teachers as a profession to be ever vigilant of the destruction of an educational tradition that (however inadequately it might have been implemented) has attributed central import-ance to the liberating force of the arts and the humanities. Furthermore, there is a need to be critical of the increasing functional role being given to schools in a technological society. Possibly what we now want is a reassertion of humanistic values and of creative and expressive powers of the mind to meet the social difficulties arising from an ever more demanding tech-nology.

At the more limited level of the school, there is clearly a need to examine the values which are often hidden in the unexamined methods of teaching, structures of authority, and modes of con-trol, and yet which correlate so strongly with educational and behavioural outcomes. The moral atmosphere of the school or classroom seems to be the key element in translating thought into action and in ensuring the personal and moral growth of the individual pupil. In particular the classroom teacher might con-sider how he or she might (1) encourage greater mutual respect between teacher and pupil and between pupil and pupil; (2) create a climate of caring and fairness; (3) ensure a sense of achievement, rather than of failure, and of personal worth; (4) develop a habit of deliberation and reflective learning; (5) introduce systematic dis-cussion of significant socio-moral issues; (6) approach learning co-operatively rather than competitively; (7) foster care for the group and eventually the wider community rather than for self-interest; and (8) increase group responsibility for decisions taken.

At a very general level personal and social education is a matter of ensuring respect for persons as I described it in chapter 2. But such a value needs to be translated into specific attitudes and procedures if the appropriate classroom ethos is to be achieved.

It would be wrong, however, if this concern for the context of the curriculum should be seen as an excuse for doing nothing about the formal, timetabled curriculum itself. To that we must now turn.

NOTES

1   See in particular Jamieson and Lightfoot (1982) *Schools and Industry*, Schools Council Working Paper 73, which is an account and evalu-ation of the project and which provides some useful case studies.

2 TVEI The Government's new technical education initiative for schools was announced by the Prime Minister to Parliament on 12 November 1982. It was to be sponsored and financed by the Manpower Services Commission (MSC), and therefore indirectly by the Department of Employment rather than by the Department of Education and Science. If the local education authorities (LEA) had been unwilling to co-operate in such a radical departure from the normal direction of and control over the curriculum of schools, then, according to its chairman David Young, the MSC would have been prepared to set up its own 14 to 18 technical high schools. In the event, local authorities did co-operate. Fourteen pilot schemes began running from September 1983, with an initial annual funding of £7 million. Each scheme was accepted by the MSC on condition that it met certain broad criteria. These might be summarised as: a coherently planned curriculum 14 to 18; equal opportunities for boys and girls; technically and vocationally orientated for about 30 per cent of the curriculum in the early years but increasing considerably beyond this; involving in its planning and execution members of the community, especially industrialists; concerned with personal effectiveness and interpersonal skills; having co-ordination of resources between institutions, especially schools and colleges; applicable to the full ability range; providing suitable work experience; leading to qualifications and further training possibilities. Although presently financed by the MSC the scheme is being run through the LEAs and it is envisaged that the whole scheme may be brought back into the educational budget.

3 A recent report by the Women's National Commission (1983) raises very clearly the issues of sex discrimination in schools – the relevance of current legislation and what further needs to be done. One should read in this connection Spender (1982) *Invisible Women: The Schooling Scandal*; Kelly (1981) *The Missing Half: Girls and Science Education*; and Chandler (1980) *Educating Adolescent Girls*. Gilligan's (1982) *In a Different Voice* applies the developmental psychology referred to in this book to women's development.

4 Nelson and Leach (1981) in a paper entitled 'Increasing opportunities for entrepreneurs' estimate that, in the USA, 80 per cent of the fifty thousand new businesses that are started each year will fail, many through poor management. And yet small businesses generate 60 per cent of all jobs. Hence, they argue, there is a need to foster those qualities of initiative and entrepreneurship that will help young persons to establish small businesses successfully.

6 Formal Curriculum

I Mapping the Territory

The issues we have been considering so far are as extensive as the educational enterprise itself. It is difficult to see how any part of the curriculum does not in some way affect a person's development. That is why I have constantly stressed the need to look at the impact upon each person of the curriculum as a whole and why we need to address ourselves to the values 'hidden' in the relationships, structures, and formal curriculum of the school.

None the less, such questions should not be an excuse for ignoring the specific contribution of planned, formal curriculum (the slots on the timetable for various subjects or activities or experiences). There are, for instance, concepts to be grasped if one is to deliberate from a moral or a political point of view; there are skills to be learnt in interpersonal problem-solving; there are attitudes to be acquired and habits to be formed. Such concepts, skills, attitudes, and habits can and should become the objectives of any deliberate, educational attempt to assist in personal and social development. There are, indeed, limitations to curriculum planning through first establishing clear objectives, but these limitations lie chiefly in narrowly interpreting 'objectives' in terms of specific behaviours. There can only be as much precision as the nature of the subject matter permits.

The matrix on page 114 is an attempt to 'map' the objectives for curriculum purposes as a result of the points and the distinctions I have made in previous chapters. It should be remembered however that, given the cross-curriculum significance of personal and social education, the objectives appropriate for the different cells of the matrix would not *necessarily* link directly with traditional school subjects.

The different elements should be treated as no more than a

check-list, a guide to school-based curriculum discussion, planning and evaluation. There can be no substitute for each school developing its own matrix and its own objectives in the light of its agreement or disagreement with the arguments in this book.

The idea of a matrix arises from work with the APU exploratory group on personal and social development (APU, 1981), although mine differs significantly from the APU's. There it was stated:

> The first major task of the group was to 'map the territory' as an essential preliminary to ascertaining what could or could not, should or should not, be assessed . . . The group concluded that personal and social development could be broken down into a series of *aspects* and *dimensions* [my italics].

(page 4)

The *dimensions* referred to: (i) factual knowledge; (ii) understanding and reasoning; (iii) attitudes; and (iv) practical application. Of course, this is a simplification in two respects. It is frequently impossible in practice to see these different dimensions of development separately: factual knowledge entails *some* understanding, and vice versa, and it is impossible to have attitudes, feelings, or emotions without some understanding of the situation. Secondly, one could argue for more distinctions. Practical application, for instance, includes habits, skills, and actual behaviours. But it should be remembered that the matrix is to serve as only a rough and ready check-list for planning and evaluation purposes.

The *aspects* of personal and social development referred, first, to those general features of development as a person and, secondly, to those more specific features which constituted what I have referred to as development as a particular sort of person. The relation between general and specific might be seen *in some cases* as the application of these more general features to specific areas of concern. Thus the more general characteristics of being a person that I talked about in chapters 2 and 3 need to be expressed in particular areas of knowing, feeling and behaving.

Such a matrix is crude, unfinished, and merely suggestive, but it sets out a framework within which one might work out in a fairly coherent way the kinds of facts, concepts, rational capacities, feelings, attitudes, habits, and skills which might enter into a school's attempt to take seriously the personal and social education of its pupils. Each school would need to fill in the cells of the matrix with its own 'interpretation' of these fairly general categories. Not all cells of course need to have objectives 'written in'

	Cognitive capacity *Note a*	Facts to be known	Attitudes, feelings, dispositions	Practical application *Note b*
A General considerations				
(i) Being a person (including the capacity for entering into personal relations) *Note c*				
(ii) Moral perspective				
(iii) Ideals (including religious and other styles of life) *Note d*				
B Specific application				
(i) Moral rules, behaviours and so on				
(ii) Social issues (a) race (b) sexism (c) nuclear war (d) environment (for example, pollution) *Note e*				
(iii) Politics (a) citizenship or membership of the state (b) community participation (c) the rule of the law				
(iv) Place within society (a) occupation (b) status and class (c) economic and social needs				
(v) Health (a) physical (b) mental				

Notes

(a) **Cognitive capacity** – this includes reasoning ability, understanding, acquisition of relevant concepts.

(b) **Practical application** – how a person actually behaves, plus habits and skills required to behave appropriately. These are distinguishable sub-categories that could appear as such if one did not mind a very complicated matrix.

(c) **Being a person** – this includes general social growth, social awareness, and so on, since, if my analysis in chapters 2 and 3 is correct, development as a person is inseparable from coming to see oneself in relation to others, coming to see things from another's point of view, and developing some sense of reciprocity and community.

(d) **Ideals** – too often personal growth is seen from a purely psychological point of view and moral growth is seen in the context of principles and duty. But the place of ideals in development, going beyond what is obligatory, needs to be explored. In a secular education, religion might be seen as one way of providing ideals that transcend the needs of everyday transactions.

(e) **Social issues** – these will no doubt change from society to society, but in our society the ones listed seem to be issues in which respect for persons, social awareness, and moral ideals have current significance. Different schools might wish to add other issues to the list.

---

to them – there may, for instance, be no specific moral facts to be known. Nor need such objectives become part of the timetabled curriculum; one may be of the opinion that certain objectives are best achieved through the relationships established between pupil and teacher, or through a particular way of exercising authority, or through extramural and residential experiences, or through pastoral organisation, or through a certain mode of teaching. The point is that if one is to take personal and social development seriously as a planned part of the curriculum, one needs a *detailed* account of what that requires and one needs to set out such an account in terms which expose it to the critical scrutiny of colleagues and of others outside the school. Then one can see whether, or where, personal and social education is happening in the curriculum and what further arrangements need to be made to ensure there are no important gaps. Where, for example, is respect for persons dealt with in the context of race or sexism, two issues of current social and moral importance?

To explore these issues, and indeed to fill the gaps which might have been revealed in the matrix, there may be a need for a school to engage in its own research – to find out, for example, what are the 'survival skills' required by young people living within that community (see B (iv) (c) in the matrix), or what personal qualities are most important to local employers, but perhaps are often lacking in the applicants for jobs (B (iv) (a) in the matrix).

In establishing the objectives teachers would need, too, to distinguish the different levels at which values enter into the very fabric of social life. At one level, the ideals of personhood within society (see (A) (iii) in the matrix) are so bound up with the values and qualities that constitute that social life, that there is little scope for *deciding* what personal development should consist in. We cannot totally step outside the particular social tradition that we have been born to and brought up in – although that tradition of social ideals and values needs protecting against erosion. For example, there are values connected with critical enquiry such as 'not cooking the books' or 'looking at conclusions in the light of evidence' which, however much we contradict them in practice (scientists do sometimes cook the books), could not seriously be denied in a society in which intellectual and investigative enquiry is a part of its way of life. Or again there are values concerning democratic ways of resolving political and social conflict which would be common to different political parties and which would constitute ideals to be upheld, transcending the differences between political parties.

At the other extreme (see B (i) in the matrix) there are qualities of character such as punctuality and self-control, virtues such as patience and generosity, and attitudes such as distrust of authority, or there are political commitments (see B (iii) in the matrix) such as Bennite socialism or Thatcherite monetarism which, although defensible, are not universally agreed upon within society and would depend upon particular moral, social, and political points of view or could even be considered a matter of taste. Different people, including headmasters, have different values and tastes at this level, and this is reflected in the various practices within schools and their differing ethos, aimed implicitly at producing different sorts of persons.

It is too big a task to fill out the cells of the matrix here, but examples of some of the cells might be:

A (i) Being a person

Cognitive capacity: This would include the ways in which one comes to see both oneself and others as persons, described in chapter 2, section 1 of this book. It would include the imaginative extension of this concept to other groups who so often have not been seen as persons.

Facts to be known: This would possibly include certain physiological and psychological facts about persons which affect our understanding of how they think and feel.

Attitudes, feelings, dispositions: This would include respect for persons as analysed in chapter 2, section 4. It would include too the developing empathy one has for others.

Practical application: This would include basic skills of interpersonal relations.

A (ii) Moral perspective

Cognitive capacity: This would include the developing capacity to think in terms of fairness and in terms of principles (see chapter 3, section 3). It would include, too, the rational and language skills referred to by Wilson (see my chapter 4, section 6).

Facts to be known: This would include those moral rules (moral content) which are generally acceptable within our society, such as not stealing or not telling lies or not hurting people for the fun of it – bearing in mind that the developing 'cognitive capacity' would change the understanding of, and therefore approach to, that moral content.

Attitudes, feelings, dispositions: This would include the disposition one has towards rules that are judged to be fair, and the connected attitude towards authority (see chapter 3, section 2, where I deal with the change from unilateral to mutual respect). It would include, too, the respect for, and empathy towards, other persons (see chapter 3, section 3).

Practical application: This would include the 'strength of character' to act according to one's principles, which might in turn involve identification with the 'moral group' which upholds those values (see chapter 2, section 3 and chapter 5, section 4).

Examples of the specific cells might be:

B (iv) Place within society

(a) *Occupation*
Cognitive capacity: This would include a working grasp of concepts relating to the world of work (apprenticeship, trade unions, industry) and the ability to apply this understanding to one's own interests, aspirations, and ability.
Facts to be known: This would include the range of jobs available, the qualifications needed for those jobs, sources of information about them.
Attitudes, feelings, dispositions: This would include how disposed one felt to different kinds of work (for example, wealth-producing as opposed to social services), or, more importantly, towards one-self and others who may no longer depend upon regular employment to give one status or a sense of importance.
Practical application: This would include relevant decision-making skills, as well as required work habits such as punctuality or clearing up one's mess.

Each of the examples I have given could be enlarged or, indeed, disputed. What is important is, first, that components of personal and social education should be spelt out and, secondly, that these components should be illustrated with detailed objectives that can become the basis of curriculum planning. Such detail will give others (colleagues, parents, the wider community) the chance to see what the school means by 'the socially and morally developed person'. It will also enable the school to see where it is doing something across the curriculum about achieving its aims. Even if a matrix is never completed by a school as part of its deliberate curriculum planning, it might help to clarify teachers' thoughts if they tried to continue what I have only tentatively begun.

2 Curriculum Areas

This is, and must be, the weakest section of the book. It aims to show how different subjects and areas of the curriculum might contribute to personal and social education. Of course each subject is worthy of a book on its own, and such a book would, amongst other things, point to further literature – textbooks, poetry, reports – through which the issues are dealt with. But, in my defence, I am here simply mapping the territory and showing in very general terms how different subjects might be seen to fit in to the overall aims of personal and social education. In doing so I wish to achieve three things: first, to indicate where further exploration by interested teachers might be undertaken – and, for that reason, I give several references; secondly, to provide a few concrete examples that deserve closer attention, and might be developed more systematically by others; thirdly, to demonstrate how these subject-specific contributions might be seen to fit in to the more general theoretical perspective developed in this book.

(i)   Humanities

(a)   *Integrated*

The main focus of subjects within the humanities area is (ideally) upon understanding what is distinctively humane about man or woman – exploring the feelings and emotions, seeing man's development through history, coming to grips with the culture that both shapes and is shaped by persons, gaining insight into human motivation, identifying the ways in which people interact with their physical and social environment, appreciating the accomplishments of mankind, fathoming the ways in which man finds meaning in life (through religion, philosophy or the arts), and appreciating the basis of the social framework and the institutions created by man. Of course, the teaching of the different subjects within the humanities – history, geography, English, religious education – may not look like that in practice. In fact it is a sad commentary upon the teaching of humanities that, in so many schools, a separate subject has been established called personal and social education, or health education, as though a primary concern of the humanities did not lie in the exploration of distinctively human areas of concern.

Two projects in the last few years have focused upon the main purposes of the humanities.

Humanities Curriculum Project 14 to 16[1]
This Schools Council Project, directed by Lawrence Stenhouse, was started in 1967. The problem it confronted was that of handling in the classroom controversial issues of practical living. The areas that became focal points of this integrated humanities course included: violence, war, authority, relations between the sexes, race, poverty. Part of being a person lies in taking a stance in relation to issues which are an inescapable part of living and in which practical decisions have to be made – even if they are decisions to follow the crowd. Yet such issues are controversial in the sense that society is divided over what one ought to do or how one might arrive at a correct decision. Part of the problem lies in the range of different sorts of consideration that might, and should, enter into the deliberations – from the perspectives of the artist, the theologian, the historian, and so on. For instance, to appreciate complex decisions in the area of war the project demonstrated how one needs to consider not only the facts of war but the different emotional responses to it, as explored by such poets as Wilfred Owen and Rupert Brooke, the theological account of the just war, the political and economic reasons for war, the glory and the horror of war. To secure this deliberation and attention to different kinds of reasoning, the teacher's role was to help pupils relate their reasoning and points of view to relevant evidence and to provide a framework in which members of the class could together consider these bits of evidence and examine their respective positions. The much discussed 'neutral role' of the teacher arose from the need to protect the deliberations from being swayed by the authority of the teacher, rather than by the authority of the evidence, and to promote reflective rather than didactic reasoning that would lead to personally significant decisions.

Man: A Course of Study (age 8 to 13)[2]
This course, associated with the theory of instruction developed by Bruner (see Bruner, 1966, chapter 4) focused on three major questions: (i) what is human about man? (ii) how did he become so? (iii) how can he become more so? The course was structured around five distinctive features of being human – prolonged child-rearing, use of tools, language, social organisation, and myth-making. Such key questions could be approached at different levels of development, but an intelligent enquiry into them

required the mastery of key ideas or concepts which became the organising structure of the course. In keeping with the importance Bruner attached to enquiry methods and to discovery learning, the course devised a series of games, simulation exercises, and activities – also excellent source material – so that the young pupil could come to see in his or her own way the significance of these key characteristics.

There are, of course, many examples of integrated humanities courses. These two (*Humanities Curriculum Project* and *Man: A Course of Study*), however, are useful because they illustrate the different ways in which humanities subjects might contribute to personal development:

(i)   they involve the exploration of values in the concrete situations of practical living, and thereby enhance the possibility of responsible decision-making and action;

(ii) they involve a shift from a dependence upon the authority of the teacher to a dependence upon the authority of evidence and reasons;

(iii) they indicate the importance of acquiring certain key concepts in understanding distinctively human qualities and capacities;

(iv) they promote certain procedural values which enhance the capacity to reason, reflect, and deliberate;

(v)   they provide a central place for the exploration and development of a 'feeling response' to human situations;

(vi) they draw upon (and show the place of) different cultural resources – poetry, anthropology, history, politics, social science, religion – in the deliberation about values and in coming to understand themselves and other persons.

In particular, however, it should be noted how an integral part of the understanding of humanistic studies in their contribution to personal development is the classroom atmosphere, the active mode of learning, the non-authoritarian relationships between teacher and pupil, and the strategies for involving pupils in deliberation and reflective learning.

The 'humanities' is too frequently however disintegrated into separate subjects, each with a syllabus to follow and a mode of instruction suitable for examinations rather than for the deliberative reflection that is required for the exploration of values. And yet such systematic reflection ought to be at the centre of humanistic studies, drawing upon the rich resources of literature and of the arts to aid young people in their enquiries. I have argued earlier (see page 66) that a concern for personal and social education needs to take seriously the values that young people have – how *they* think and feel about matters of personal and social importance, what their consuming interests are – if that 'selection from the culture' that schools make possible is to enter into their lives in any significant way. How can we place this exploration of values within the context of the humanities where it belongs, unless there is some relaxation of the rigid boundaries which divide one subject from another?

(b)   Topics: racism, sexism, peace

Three topics, for example, where general features of personal development need to be applied across subject boundaries to concrete cases are those of racism, sexism, and nuclear war (see B (ii) (a), (b), (c) in the matrix on page 114). The humanities, in drawing upon the resources of history and literature, is the place where matters of such personal and social importance should become the focus of systematic and reflective thinking. The most important issue we must face as a society is that of racism and of how to live in harmony and respect with people of different backgrounds and cultures. There are many aspects of this and an understanding of them requires not only an historical perspective but a cross-cultural one, too, and an appreciation through literature of what it is like to be a member of a minority group, often the victim of others' prejudices. Further, there is a need to explore the deeper psychological forces of prejudice and hatred, which influence attitudes and behaviours beyond the issues of race though most powerfully at work within that context, and the relation of these forces to one's own, very often insecure, identity and self-image. The curriculum problems here are illustrated in the history of the *Humanities Curriculum Project* race pack, which, in assisting the pupils to explore their own attitudes and prejudices and to exercise a more reasoned approach to what was so often unreasoned, fell foul of the Schools Council and the materials were never published. Stenhouse did subsequently obtain money to build on the work pioneered by the *Humanities Curriculum Project* in exploring classroom strategies for handling questions of race. Three approaches were adopted: the selection of a balanced set of evidence as a basis for open-ended discussion under the chairmanship of the teacher; the promotion of a positive anti-racist stance; and the use of simulation and role play to act out the feelings and situations. A full account of the project is given in Stenhouse *et al.* (1982).

Similar problems arise over sex stereotyping and the hidden values purveyed through social attitudes and practices. How can these be explored on the curriculum? Clearly they need to be because a boy or girl's attitude to sex roles will affect the sort of person he or she becomes and the sort of relationships that are subsequently established. There are, of course, facts to be known concerning the openings to girls which, through recent legislation, have been made possible. But there are deeper questions about attitudes and aspirations and image of oneself as man or woman which have to be explored, requiring an insight into feelings and an historical perspective that only a sensitively taught humanities course can bring. None the less, there is now a literature which helps the teacher to handle these issues in the curriculum.[3]

(c)   Religious education

One subject which traditionally has accepted responsibility for personal and social development is religious education. For many the connection between religion and morality has seemed self-evident. Such a connection between the two, however, has been challenged by many, including Hirst (1965 and 1974) who argues that religion and morality are logically different ways of interpreting experience. Indeed, in an increasingly secular society where only a minority would be swayed by religious consider-ations, it would be mistaken from the practical point of view (irrespective of any philosophical considerations) to make moral development depend on religious belief. None the less, recent developments have understood religious education much more broadly than the 'confessional approach' that prevailed in the past. Cox (1983), for instance, explains that the purpose of religious education is to convey an understanding of the experiences and the emotions that underlie the acquisition of human values. Hull (1982), too, links religious education with the central human task, characteristic of all cultures, of searching for meaning.

There are problems, however, in this interpretation of religion, and these are explored in various ways by Niblett (1960) and O'Hare (1978). What is to be valued and how life should be lived cannot be discussed, let alone made sense of, in a form of discourse totally insulated from background beliefs about social relations, human nature, and growth as a person. And religious beliefs must be a very important part of this background. To believe that one has an eternal destiny or that one has been made in the 'image and likeness of God' fills out the meaning of 'personhood' in a way that affects what counts as respect for persons or growth as a person or, indeed, where the cut-off between persons and non-persons is to occur. Related concepts of 'dignity', 'freedom', 'autonomy' take on a changed meaning, and different orders of priority will be given to qualities upheld as virtues.

(d)   History

The relevance of particular subjects within the humanities to the exploration of values and to a 'feeling response' that transcends subject boundaries is increasingly recognised in developments within subject areas – for example, the Schools Council projects *Geography for the Young School Leaver* and *History 13 to 16*. History has of course always played a significant part in upholding the ideals, myths and values of society as Musgrave (1982, page 70) says:

> For as long as history has been taught in schools there has been a series of aims, moral in nature, in the minds of teachers. The stories of national heroes, Nelson or Florence Nightingale, have been taught in the hope that they would be seen as moral exemplars. Great victories, for example that of Drake over the Spanish Armada, have been emphasised in the hope of building patriotism.

These and similar points are explored by Ward (1975). Lest, however, we think that such a view of history is a thing of the past, we have recently been reminded by the Secretary of State for Education and Science of the purpose of history. He was criticising the proposed criteria for the syllabuses and examination of the joint GCE/CSE examinations at 16+, submitted by the history panel (see *The Times Educational Supplement* 15 April 1983):

> One of the aims of studying history is to understand the development of shared values which are a distinctive feature of British society and culture and which continue to shape private attitudes and public policy.

Facing History and Ourselves

This Project, directed by Margot Stern-Strom and Bill Parsons, began in 1976 in two junior high schools in Brookline, Massachusetts. The title is revealing. The Nazi holocaust is a piece of history in living memory of many people. Part of the historical evidence can be the first-hand accounts of those who survived. It is also a piece of history where complex facts need to be acquired and pieced together, where evidence is rich and varied, and where there are different interpretations needing to be reconciled with the facts. For our purposes it confronts the student with a situation in which normal human values are abandoned by people who would otherwise be regarded as educated and civilised, in which the relation of individual motivation and interests to social pressures and values needs to be explained, and in which institutional and group self-interest vies with personal survival. It is important that we do not forget the holocaust. But it is important, too, that our memory is rooted in critical understanding and that we see that even this, the most horrifying of historical events, happened recently and within a social context that could be re-enacted by ordinary people such as we mix with every day. As Kuhmerker (1981) observed in introducing the project:

> We want future generations to be neither victims nor victimisers, so each generation has to learn that human beings can and do make choices. There are times for making choices and times when the choices of others must be resisted; otherwise human beings may find themselves facing choice-less choice.

None the less, the teaching of the Holocaust Project (given its aims) needs to respect the developmental stages of middle adolescence. A curriculum must, if the arguments of this book are correct, have a developmental perspective as well as an academically defensible content. Central to the Holocaust Project therefore are questions of obedience, loyalty and obligation, for as Strom (1981) argues:

> . . . the lives of early adolescents are centred in peer groups and mutual relationship. The students are likely to be struggling with issues of loyalty, trust, and responsibility as individuals within groups.

The project material is published in textbook[4] and provides resources for examining the holocaust and the psychological and economic circumstances that led to it. It is well researched, and the references to further writings and to historical evidence are plentiful for the scholarly student who wishes to check the facts or pursue the enquiry further. But there is a pattern to the presentation. The unit

. . . builds upon the concepts of conflict and conflict resolution, powers, leadership, obedience, resistance, and justice. We see these as the themes common to all study of history which aims to make connections between past events and the lives of students.

(Strom, 1981, page 9)

Indeed, as we said with Kohlberg, one of the chief ways in which students develop a higher level of thinking is that of having to resolve conflicts – of finding difficulties in the simple answer. As this material demonstrates (at least when handled properly by the teacher) there is no simple answer to explaining the facts of the holocaust, even though the holocaust itself might have been seen by its perpetrators as a simple answer to their problems.

The US Department of Education has recognised the Holocaust Project as 'an exemplary model education project worthy to be disseminated and adopted across the country'. It has now been adopted in over thirty different school settings in five States.

(e)   Literature

The central place of literature in the exploration of values, the refinement of feeling, and the understanding of the human condition has been constantly stressed by, among others, Bantock (1955, 1963, 1965, 1967), drawing upon a tradition associated with Arnold, Leavis, and Eliot. Indeed, in the absence of this cultural tradition made accessible through the curriculum, the current vogue for self-expression or social and life skills is notable in its superficiality. Literature enables the universal concerns to be explored and examined vividly through the vicarious experience and challenges superficial analyses and simple solutions. In the introduction to his recent book, *The Parochialism of the Present*, Bantock states:

Briefly it is time we recovered a sense of history; and within a resuscitated awareness of historic process, it is time we recalled a literature as a central energising force in the examination of our social and moral problems (among which of course, education has a prominent place).

The place of literature and the arts in the refinement of the emotions and in the moral education of young people has been a constant theme in Bantock's many contributions to education. And it provides a challenge to the rather rationalist and programmed approach to personal development which, in parts, this book may be guilty of. Under the influence of Kant, we have perhaps found the life of feeling a bit of a nuisance in personal development rather than its very core. Indeed, some would argue that 'the refinement of the emotions' and 'moral education' is a false distinction. Certainly my brief account of dispositions in chapter 4, section 4 is far from adequate. Bantock takes exception to the narrow rationalist basis upon which so many recent accounts of moral decision-making are constructed. He gives an example from *Wuthering Heights* where the basis of morality, upon which decisions are arrived at, is more (quoting Iris Murdock) 'attached to the substance of the world', suggesting 'an order of reality where purely rational considerations are irrelevant.'

The whole experience of *Wuthering Heights* seems to me to indicate forces at work in the effect of one personality on another which the rationalist either ignores or shudders away from.

(Bantock, 1967, page 144)

Of course, literature has so often been used to promote specific values – Arthur Ransome's tales making desirable a certain kind of adventurous and plucky personality, or Rudyard Kipling's poems stressing tough moral qualities (see Musgrave, 1982). Some of these might seem rather obvious and superficial – precisely for this reason Enid Blyton's stories were banned as dangerous from some libraries! – but this need not be so. There is now a wide range of stories for young children that extend social awareness into a variety of topics and explore qualities that are of concern to young children (for example, those of laziness, greed, and discontent, as they are dealt with in Berg's *Folk Tales for Reading and Telling*). Dickens' *Fly away Peter* deals with two unusual friends attracted to each other by their abnormalities and helping each other to overcome their respective problems; even the 'Mister Men' series deals with significant qualities in personal development (see Evans, 1982). The list is endless. It is important however for teachers at infant and junior levels to make collections of stories and poems which deal in an attractive way with themes that are significant to the children's development.[5]

At secondary level the connection between literature and development need hardly be made to the teacher of English whose main task is to introduce young people to a very rich literary tradition. The significance of literature is identified by Willey (1964):

> . . . if we admit that literary judgments are often disguised (or
> undisguised) ethical judgments, or that they presuppose such
> judgments, then we ought to be enquiring into the nature and
> history of moral ideas.

Writers who have explored the connection between English
teaching and personal development are Abbs (1976), and Hildick
(1970).

(ii)   Social Studies

The boundary between humanities and social studies is indeed
rather arbitrary, but the distinction is made in practice. Social
studies would include the study of the individual in society in so
far as this draws upon the social sciences of sociology, social
psychology, psychology, economics, and politics. The relevance
of such studies to personal, social and moral education as it has
been developed in this book and as it has been mapped out in the
matrix (see page 114) should be fairly clear, although often aspects
of social studies are taught as if they in no way affect the development of personal values. The capitalist assumptions behind economics courses, for example, are rarely themselves questioned – and
therefore particular social values are implicitly transmitted unexamined. Lee (1974), however, in his interesting contribution to
Whitehead's collection of essays does begin to examine this hidden
aspect of economics teaching.

The most thorough summary of different approaches to social
education is provided by Rosemary Lee in her FEU (1980b) report
Beyond Coping. Quoting James Hemming (1949), Lee (page 7)
demonstrates the gradiose aims that have at times been set for
social studies:

> To foster the development of spontaneity, self-reliance, flexibil-
> ity of mind, clear thinking tolerance, initiative, articulateness,
> adventurousness of outlook, courage in the face of new prob-
> lems, enjoyment of created activitiy, sound standards of action
> and appreciation, world-mindedness, a sense of purpose and a
> philosophy of life.

Obviously the completely developed person! But social studies
has never lived up to such aims and has frequently become a
section of the curriculum reserved for low achievers.

Lawton and Dufour (1973) provided a new rationale for social
studies – an academically respectable analysis (drawing upon the

social sciences) of the social environment within which people develop as persons and as citizens. Such development and the adoption of social responsibility required knowledge and the understanding of relevant concepts and principles. The danger in this however might lie in an over-academic approach to issues which are of immediate personal concern and to which young people themselves might have a significant contribution to make based on their own experience (see Gleeson and Whitty, 1976).

One area within social studies is of particular significance for personal and social education – political education (see page 114, B (iii) in the matrix). An important feature of personal development stressed in the first part of this book is that of gradually taking on responsibility for one's own decisions as well as respecting the ability of others to establish their own priorities. Responsibility and respect affect the social arrangements that are made between individuals, and it is the mark of a well run society that such arrangements are institutionalised so as to ensure the maximum responsibility to, and respect for, each member. The capacity to participate in and to contribute to such a society, however, needs to be developed, and yet so rarely is within schools. Political education requires: (i) knowledge about the institutions and procedures within society (both national and more local ones); (ii) those concepts through which one might understand social processes from a political angle; and (iii) the 'know-how' – the practical ability – to participate in a political form of life. Indeed, the development of such understanding and know-how should be at the centre of our curriculum, for without them the democratic ideals we value are in danger of being subverted – from the extreme right as well as from the extreme left. As youth unemployment hits an ever-increasing number of school leavers, a docile acceptance of their lot will very likely turn into angry confrontation, alienated as they will be from the institutions and social arrangements which have placed them where they are, unless they are politically and actively involved in the processes which shape their community. There is indeed a considerable literature now on political education, identifying those key ideas which are the basis of political understanding.[6]

There is however a danger in this emphasis upon political literacy, and this is suggested by Porter (1979):

> . . . political literacy would be limited to a solitary intellectual exercise; the politically literate person would merely be capable

of well-informed observation and analysis. The ultimate test of effective political education lies in creating a proclivity to action.

But to create such a 'proclivity to action' requires treating young people as 'political animals' even from a young age, engaging them in those decisions which affect the distribution of power and resources, shifting them from an attitude of unilateral to mutual respect towards authority, giving them a sense of power within the institutions (such as school) to which they belong. All this, of course, requires an attitude towards and a policy for the treatment of young people that goes beyond a subject on the curriculum. Kohlberg's 'just community' school described on pages 105–7 was an exercise in political education.

(iii)   Health Education

One area of the curriculum that, in the decline of religious education, is increasingly claiming responsibility for personal and social education is 'health education'. How this has happened is interesting. 'Health' seems on the surface to be an unambiguous term. To be healthy means to be free of diseases, fit and able to take an active part in games and social activities, not getting tired too quickly or easily, being less vulnerable to colds and infections. Health education, therefore, would consist in transmitting the knowledge that enabled young people to remain healthy. Its content would obviously have a central place for knowledge about the body, how it functions and what exercise and nourishment it requires. The subject becomes more complex when it gets into the area of mental health.

What, however, is frequently not made clear is the evaluative meaning of 'health'. What counts as a healthy form of life, even physical life, is a matter of taste and value. I am not sure, for instance, that the Americans young or old who, as I wrote parts of this book, sweated and panted without ceasing past my window in pursuit of *health* are in fact (by my standards) living a more healthy life. Furthermore, the concern for health becomes very quickly tied up with moral issues. For example, sexually transmitted diseases are quite obviously instances of ill-health but they also raise important moral questions about sexual relations. Drugs affect the body's functioning, but they too raise questions about what is desirable from a social and moral point of view. Health education, therefore, has extended its area of concern into personal, social and moral education, often however without questioning its credentials for doing so – or the qualifications of health education for guiding young people in these matters. To establish health education as a subject quite separate from the humanities is in danger of placing personal, social and moral issues outside the cultural traditions represented by the humanities through which these issues need to be understood and examined. The problems are illustrated by the Schools Council projects *Health Education 5 to 13* and *13 to 18*, which given central importance to three related ideas. These are summarised by Williams and Williams (1981) as follows:

(i)   the notion of 'health career' based upon a belief that the health-behaviour of individuals is likely to have a history of development in the sense of there being an interconnected labyrinth of knowledge, values, beliefs, attitudes, expectations and experience through the growth and development of individuals;

(ii)   the importance of helping children and young people to recognise and accept that their health is largely a personal responsibility; inherent in this lies the importance of decision-making skills concerning health-related behaviour;

(iii) the importance of the images that children have of themselves (self-concept) in influencing their behaviour in many circumstances, particularly in their relationships with others.

To help explore these ideas the projects aim, through their materials and suggested activities and experiences, to provide:

(i)   knowledge of health related information and skills of enquiry and recall;

(ii)   skills of analysis, synthesis, and evaluation of health related information;

(iii) clarification of values, feelings and attitudes related to particular health information or issues – both of oneself and of others;

(iv) investigating possible alternative behaviours and their outcomes related to specifice health issues;

(v)   deciding upon an appropriate course of action for 'myself'.

These general ideas and the main aims are spelt out in the projects in terms of eight main content areas, which could provide the basis of systematic curriculum development within the school. I do not doubt the value of this, nor the good work that has certainly been initiated in schools arising from the projects. I do however, have three worries about these developments: first, the ambiguous notion of health which on the one hand trades upon the scientific sense of a properly functioning organism and on the other hand takes on board the range of personal, social and moral issues raised in this book; secondly, the isolation of these personal, social and moral issues from the wider cultural framework within which they need to be examined critically; and thirdly, the all-embracing concerns of what is but one small area of the curriculum.

The extent of health education interests is reflected in Balding's (1983) health related behaviour questionnaire which is increasingly being employed in schools. Those interested in this and other developments in health education should read *Education and Health*, the Journal of the Schools Health Education Unit, Exeter University.[7]

(iv)   Expressive Arts

Bantock (1971) advocated two sorts of curriculum, one for those who were able to read, enjoy, and benefit from an essentially literary culture, and one for those who, whatever their native wit, felt much more at home in a culture where feelings were expressed (and could be explored) much more effectively through dance, drama, and the arts. This distinction came in for a great deal of criticism, especially the divisive nature of what was sometimes referred to as 'the all-singing, all-dancing curriculum' for the working class. The more positive aspects however of the place of the expressive arts at the centre of education for personal development received little attention. It is interesting to see, therefore, that Hargreaves (1982), approaching curriculum problems from a different perspective, does himself attach so much importance in his suggested common-core curriculum to the expressive arts, especially drama.

The general argument is that an essential feature of personal growth is the development and refinement of a 'feeling response' to oneself, to others, and to the environment. Such a development frequently gets neglected in the intellectual/academic nature of the curriculum and in the priority we attach to propositional knowledge and to 'getting things correct'. There are however different 'languages' – and different functions of language from that of getting the 'right answer'. Furthermore certain 'languages' (those of music or of art or of drama) are more suited to making sense out of experience and to making intelligible, both to ourselves and to others, how we feel. On the other hand, too much emphasis upon self-expression has distracted us from the cognitive aspect of our feelings (the affective is so often seen as something quite separate from the cognitive, and indeed something which gets in the way of educational progress) and has thus distracted us, too, from the educational task of refining our emotions and feelings as a form of knowing. Reid (1969), following Susan Langer, emphasises the development of 'meaning' through the arts, and criticises the way in which the dominance of mathematics and of science has given us a distorted view of what counts as knowledge. Arguing in a similar vein, Witkin (1974) talks about the intelligence of feeling, and it is interesting to note that this book provides a rationale for arts for the adolescent (see Ross, 1975).

(v) Other Subjects

It is clear that many other subjects contribute in their various ways to personal and social education, but this is not the place to examine these contributions in any detail. The sciences might on the surface appear not to make such a contribution – they are concerned with knowledge about the material world and not with values or with attitudes towards the world. There are, however, two ways in which science might make a direct contribution. First, implicit in science are certain values: that getting at the truth and not distorting the evidence matter, that one's views need to be subjected to the critical scrutiny of others, that reasons and evidence should be given for what one holds to be true, that progress requires co-operation and teamwork, that 'truth' is a common rather than a personal property. Secondly, the social and political implications of science and of technological advance are increasingly seen to be part of science education. Indeed what science is studied might, for the majority who do not aspire to continue science at an advanced level, preferably be selected on the basis of relevance to practical, political or social issues. Recently, however, the Secretary of State for Education in reviewing the proposed criteria for the joint CSE/GCE examination in physics rejected the sections concerned with the social relevance of science and technology, despite the arguments from HM Inspectorate, professional associations, industrialists and curriculum development bodies which all argued that science syllabuses should emphasise the wider social and economic implications of the subject (see *The Times Educational Supplement*, 18 March 1983).

Physical education has so often emphasised certain values and, like health education and social studies, has at times made big claims for its contribution to personal and social education. According to McIntosh (1974, page 1) in a book significantly titled *Fair Play*:

> In the modern world, therefore, an investigation of sports and pastimes may shed light not only on the characters of particular peoples but also on the character of all mankind.

Fair play, team spirit, respect for rules, courage, perseverance, endurance – these and many other qualities have at different times been seen as the hoped for outcomes of physical education. Whether or not they are in fact the outcomes is not so easy to discover. What, however, so often seem to be the values built into the exercise of games are those of physical prowess, of competition, of winning, of aggression, and of strict discipline under the rather powerful authority of the teacher or trainer. Possibly, however, the most interesting innovation in physical education that turns these values upside-down and could make a most significant contribution to personal and social education is the project directed by Martin Underwood at Exeter University. Values quite overtly stressed are 'helping each other', 'non-aggression', and 'responsibility for tasks set'. Pupils are taught not to depend upon directions of the teacher; they adjust the equipment to their own capacities, and above all they assist each other in overcoming their respective difficulties. Early evaluations show a remarkable change in attitude towards helpfulness, responsibility, and co-operation.

(vi)   Community Studies/Service (CSS)

Oliver (1976) in his book *Education and Community* starts by pointing to the 'loss of faith in the liberal vision of the modern democratic society'. Previously it was felt that, with more sophisticated social planning and with the help of modern technology, many of our social problems – especially of inequalities of wealth and of welfare – would be overcome. Education would provide the individual with the knowledge and skills that were needed to cope with life's problems (reflected in the constant emphasis upon autonomy in the aims of education) and at the same time would provide society with the skilled manpower to run a complex industrial society. Indeed, this remains the theme of public documents that look critically at schools whose activities do not seem entirely geared either to the acquisition of individual knowledge and skills or to the manpower needs of our economy. Fortunately, however, teachers retain a more complex picture of personal and social development. An underlying theme of this book has been the importance of 'community' in personal growth. This can be seen at two levels. First, the emphasis in educational philosophy upon equality and freedom has led to the neglect of that third important element, 'fraternity' or community as a value. Secondly, a sense of community and reciprocity seems to be an important element in promoting the personal growth we talked about in Part I. Indeed, I would argue that top priority in personal and social education should be given to creating that sense of community within the school and between school and those outside the school. Oliver's answer to the crises that are now occurring in large complex industrial societies is to resurrect the sense of community on a scale that individuals can make sense of, identify with, and participate in.

The connection between education, community, and quality of life, underpins many of the attempts to place CSS on the curriculum – although as Scrimshaw (1981) shows from a small evaluation of such courses in just three schools this is interpreted very widely. He sets out (on page 8) in tabular form a useful analysis of the major variable factors relevant to CSS programmes.

We can identify several major reasons why CSS has appeared on the curriculum. First, it can be seen as a soft option for low achieving youngsters – local study, and the activities that go with it, will seem more relevant. It is hoped that there will be a spin-off in terms of the pupils' motivation and sense of responsibility. And indeed this so often seems to be the case. The comment quoted by Scrimshaw (page 21) is not untypical, as many teachers of CSS will agree:

> We learned that old people were just as interesting as young people. It was nice to know that some of the lonely ones thought you were nice to talk to. You were just a new friend. It was certainly worth doing from my point of view. I found I was much more patient with old people than I thought . . . I found

myself at ease with them. I thought I'd be nervous, just being plonked with strangers, certainly not my age group. It was just fantastic – very enjoyable.

Secondly, however, there is a view that such studies will provide an opportunity for all students to develop positive attitudes and a sense of responsibility towards others less fortunate than themselves. For example, again to take an excerpt from Scrimshaw

. . . I would like to think that I might have done something during my school life to help the community however small. So far in my life the community has always given and I would like to think I have given something back.

(page 22)

Finally, it is argued that schools should create a sense of community, and that this will make it an important agent for transforming the society outside the school into a more humane community. Examples of such a view would be those presented by Midwinter (1972 and 1975) and Boyd (1977), and CSS would play a significant part in the core curriculum of such schools.

The different ways in which CSS contributes to this changing idea of how individuals and schools relate to society is traced by Ball and Ball (1973). But the title of their book, *Education for a Change?*, reflects the potential they attribute to CSS for achieving what they see to be central educational aims. Community involvement as a means ultimately of changing the community was, too, the major aim behind the Schools Council Project *Social Education: An Experiment in Four Secondary Schools* (see Rennie *et al.*, 1974).

Certainly the growth of CSS has introduced into schools many agencies from outside the schools and these have enabled pupils to gain experience that they otherwise would not have – Task Force and Community Service Volunteers to name but two. But a criticism that might be levelled against such activities is that, too frequently, they are not followed up with the systematic reflection required for them to be of *educational* significance. This criticism, however, is being met, partly as a result of CSS becoming part of the examination structure, partly of course because teachers are seeing the force of the criticism, and partly because resource material is being made available that helps teachers to approach CSS more systematically. Community Service Volunteers, for example, provides topic-based material and guides on organising community service, specimen syllabuses, resources available, and suitable contacts.

3 Retrospect: Subjects and Co-ordinated Planning

This hasty run through timetabled subjects is indeed superficial, but it aims to do three things. First, it aims to remind readers that there is a content to personal and social education and that different subjects do make their own respective contributions to that content. Indeed, with a co-ordinated approach across the different subject departments there seems little reason for a separate subject to meet the developmental aims I introduced in Part I and this is the impression of HMI with regard to personal development:

> Teachers need a view of the school curriculum as a whole and the part they play in it if they are to co-ordinate their pupils' learning and provide them with some sense of coherence in their programmes . . . Pupils need a range of experiences which in practice is provided through the subjects in the timetable. But if these subjects are to contribute more effectively to the broad education of the pupils many specialist teachers will have to break away from the isolation in which they commonly work.
> There is a further need for their doing so. Teachers generally acknowledge the need to provide more personal education in the curriculum of all pupils by including careers education, health education and political education and by stimulating awareness of economic realities and social obligations. How far this might require the development of new and special courses, and how far these needs might be better met by shifts of emphasis and content within existing subjects requires careful consideration. Some elements of what is wanted are already provided within existing examination subject syllabuses and more may be possible in future. Subjects can be interpreted in various ways to meet identified needs but only if the subject specialists have consulted and planned together with the pupils' overall programme in mind.   (DES/HMI, 1979, page 42)

Sections 1 and 2 of this chapter, therefore, need to be taken together: first, I give some overall idea of the strands of development entering into personal and social education and the different components of it; secondly, I examine how existing subjects do (or could) make their own distinctive contribution.

Secondly, such a brief reference to timetabled areas of the formal curriculum aims to show the kinds of questions that subject teachers might be asking about their own subject and the sources they might go to in their own respective enquiries. The contribution of individual subjects to personal and social education as I have outlined it would in each case make a major book in itself.

Thirdly, however, this summary aims to show the dangers arising from not having a co-ordinated approach. Not only is there a great deal of overlap – similar ground being covered in health education, home economics, and social studies – but subjects (like health education) take in problems and issues, especially in the area of practical living, which would be more at home within traditional areas of the curriculum such as the humanities.

NOTES

1   **Humanities Curriculum Project**   The project, directed by Lawrence Stenhouse from 1967–1972 at CARE, University of East Anglia, offers to teachers stimulus, support and materials appropriate to enquiry-based courses which cross the traditional boundaries between English, history, geography, religious studies, and social studies. Age range: 14 to 16.
Books and materials: Schools Council/Nuffield Humanities Project (1970) introduces the basic theory and classroom strategy. The enquiry packs (on education, family, living in cities, relations between the sexes, people and work, poverty, law and order, and war and society) contained: (1) students' element made up of around two hundred items (twenty sets of each) of printed evidence; (2) teacher's box, with examples of each item from students' element plus a handbook and index of materials; (3) tapes.
Evaluation reports are to be found in various CARE Occasional Publications. They include: Elliott and MacDonald (1975) *People in Classrooms*; Verma (1980) 'The impact of innovation', in *Towards Judgment I*; MacDonald (1969) 'Experience of innovation', in *Towards Judgment II*. Humble and Simons (1978) *From Council to*

Classroom: an evaluation of the diffusion of Humanities Curriculum Project should also be read.

2 **MACOS** A full account of *Man: A Course of Study* is given by Jenkins (1976) in units 14–15 of the Open University E 203 curriculum course. Another useful account is that of Rudduck (1972) in the Cambridge Journal of Education.

3 (a) **Racism and multi-cultural education** The following are useful background reading and curriculum sources: Taylor (1981) *Caught Between*, a review of research into the education of pupils of West Indian origin; Stone (1981) *The Education of the Black Child*; The Runnymede Trust (1980) *Britain's Black Population*; Rampton Report (1981) *West Indian Children in our Schools*; Milner (1975) *Children and Race*; House of Commons Home Affairs Committee (1981) *Racial Disadvantage*; James and Jeffcoate (1981) *The School in the Multicultural Society*; Husband (1982) *'Race' in Britain*; Willey (1982) *Teaching in Multicultural Britain*; Craft *et al.* (1982) *Teaching in a Multi-cultural Society*; Little and Willey (1981) *Multi-ethnic Education: the way forward*; Hicks (1981) *Minorities: a teacher's resource book for the multi-ethnic curriculum*; Dixon (1977) *Catching them Young Volume I: Sex, Race and Class in Children's Fiction*.

(b) **Sexism:** See chapter 5, Note 3, page 111. For a more direct concern with teaching about sex discrimination or with confronting sex discrimination on the curriculum one should refer to the Schools Council Project *Reducing Sex Differentiation in School*. Materials, reports and newsletters can be obtained from School Curriculum Development Committee, Newcombe House, 45 Notting Hill Gate, London, W11 3JB.

(c) **Peace:** A list of relevant material is obtainable from Teachers for Peace Book List, Housemans, 5 Caledonian Road, London N1 9DX. One valuable project that raises so many of the issues is the *World Studies* Project which has an abundance of resources, handbooks for teachers, a quarterly journal with some contributions on peace education, and various interim reports (Schools Council Project *World Studies 8 to 13*). Hicks (1982) raises the key issues and provides lots of practical guidance. There are teaching games from Pax Christi, St Francis of Assisi Centre, Pottery Lane, London W11 4NG and a *Gamesters' Handbook* which contains one hundred and forty games for teachers by Brandes and Phillips (1979).

4 The textbook is: Strom and Parsons (1982) *Facing History and Ourselves*. The following chapter titles indicate the topics covered: 'Society and the individual'; 'Individual decisions can alter the course of human and cultural development'; 'A case study in prejudice'; 'A German history World War I to World War II'; 'Nazi philosophy and policy'; 'Preparing for obedience'; 'Victims of tyranny'; 'Human behaviour in extreme situations'; 'Judgment'; 'Preconditions of genocide'; 'Facing today and the future'.

5 For a long annotated list of literature for young children that has been found helpful by teachers in developing social awareness in young children see Goodall *et al.* (1983).

6 **Political education** There is a lot of valuable literature now on political education. Giving a theoretical background is Crick and Porter (1978) *Political Education and Political Literacy*; Crick and Heater (1977) *Essays on Political Education*; Heater and Gillespie (1981) *Political Education in Flux*. The Hansard Society (1974–77) has produced a number of valuable papers – a programme for political education, political literacy, basic concepts and procedural values, issues and problems. Stradling (1978) has published *Political Education in the 11 to 16 Curriculum*. A developmental approach, in keeping with the general argument of this book, is provided by Greenstein (1965) in *Children and Politics* and by Tomlinson (1975) who provides a cognitive developmental perspective related to the work of Kohlberg and Piaget. Ponton and Gill (1983) have written a valuable introduction to politics; but the best source of references is Curriculum Review Unit (1983).

7 Under its Director, John Balding, the Health Education Council's Schools Health Education Unit (School of Education, University of Exeter) is involved in two major projects. The Health Related Behaviour Questionnaire service offers secondary schools a profile of pupils' behaviours covering a very wide range of activities in school, at home, and with friends; by the end of 1983 about 30,000 pupils between the age of 12 and 18 had responded. The second project is developing questionnaires to aid curriculum planning in the areas of health and social education in primary and middle schools.

7 Care and Guidance

1 Pastoral Care

Recent years have seen a rapid growth within maintained schools of a new and distinctive area of organisation, with its own career structure, professional organisation and (now) journals[1] – that of pastoral care. The reasons for this development are not hard to see. The responsibility that schools have for the wider personal and social development of young people, together with the increasing difficulty of maintaining close personal contact in very big schools, has required a more formal structure and a more explicit ascription of responsibilities. Unfortunately big organisations seem to require this.

Furthermore, teachers are having to take on responsibilities that are often more concerned with social welfare than with education. Why is that? First, schools are frequently the only places where children who are suffering from a wide range of social and medical disadvantages can find someone who is caring and intelligent to talk to and to get help from. Little do the general public know how much time and energy teachers give to sorting out personal and social difficulties that, strictly speaking, are not the responsibility of an *educational* institution at all. But someone has to do it. Secondly, a pre-condition of successful teaching is that the learners have the pre-conditions for successful learning. And this will require attendance to physical as well as emotional needs. A child who arrives hungry, cold and wet is not likely to perform well in French lessons; nor is the child who is depressed by conflicts at home likely to respond to a system that has no understanding of or sympathy with his or her personal problems. But understanding and sympathy require knowledge of the situation by the teacher and a relationship with the child that goes beyond that of instructor. Thirdly, the world that young people are entering into is an increasingly complex one in which they will need guidance. The kinds of jobs and careers available, and the variety of educational and training routes open to young people, have changed beyond recognition in recent years. It is a full-time job keeping track of these changes and being equipped to advise and inform young people so that they make sensible and realistic choices.

'Pastoral care' is the label used for meeting some of these problems. There are two major senses in which it is used. First, it refers to the responsibilities that a school assumes in helping young people to cope with personal difficulties or decisions. Secondly, it refers to the formal structures that are sometimes created which enable the school to fulfil these responsibilities. An important area of debate is whether the assumption of these rather general and ill-defined responsibilities by the school requires pastoral care in the second sense, namely, some formal arrangements. The question, in a nutshell, is this: does not the whole of the curriculum contribute to personal development and to preparation for adult life? And is it not the job, therefore, of all teachers, in so far as they foster the values and powers of the mind that we have spoken about in this book, to assume pastoral responsibilities for young people in their care? Many teachers find the distinction between pastoral care and curriculum obnoxious. And, indeed, the major theme of this book is that personal, social and moral development requires a 'cross-curriculum policy', concerning not only the impact of the curriculum as a whole upon each child but also the specific contribution each subject might make to relevant knowledge, understanding, attitudes, skills, and habits.

There are, however, three ways in which 'pastoral responsibility' might be considered to require some quite distinctive formal arrangements. These are: (i) response to individual 'crises'; (ii) vocational guidance; and (iii) anticipation of those 'problems, decisions, and adjustments' that any young person is likely to have to deal with.

(i)   Response to crises

There will inevitably be in any large group of people certain individuals who have difficulties in adjusting to the social environment in which they are obliged to spend their time. This in particular will be the case in very large schools. They will manifest behaviours which the classroom teacher will not have the time or skills or knowledge to cope with. Expert help will be needed – the experienced counsellor, the psychological advisory service, various branches of the social services when the behavioural problems are connected with social problems outside the school. There is a need therefore to have some expertise and arrangement within a school whereby individual pupils might be put in touch with those social and counselling services which are not part of the school's normal responsibility. Often this expertise and these arrangements are formalised in a house system so that the classroom teacher can refer individuals to house tutors, who often hold positions of responsibility within the secondary school.

There are dangers, however, in these arrangements, and it is important that they should be kept to a minimum. It is essentially a trouble-shooting operation – one where the normal educational functions of the school are breaking down and where a crisis has arisen that needs to be dealt with by other than educational means. There is a temptation to treat as crises situations that in fact require no special expertise; they arise within the school, possibly because of the disjunction between the curriculum and pupil needs. This, of course, is easier to say than to act upon. But I have argued in this book that personal and social education requires careful study of the hidden values of the curriculum, of the kind of relationships between pupils and those in authority, and of the impact of the curriculum as a whole upon the self-esteem and self-image of the pupils. There is a danger of shifting too readily the responsibility for behavioural problems from the social context of the school or classroom, where those problems arise, to the home or to other situations outside the school. There are remarkable differences between schools in the range of behavioural difficulties and in the way punishment is meted out, as indeed Rutter *et al.* (1979) demonstrate, even where these schools seem roughly comparable in social environment and pupil intake. Too little attention is paid in schools and in the training of teachers to what, in chapter 5, was referred to as 'classroom atmosphere' or to what, also in chapter 5, was called 'the just community'. Perhaps it is to these that more systematic attention needs to be paid in meeting the pastoral needs of pupils – and this would treat crisis situations as essentially educational ones rather than as 'individual referrals'.

(ii) Vocational guidance

Young people need help to make choices that will affect their future lives. These choices begin at a young age, formally, when they choose which set of options to take at the ages of thirteen or fourteen, informally, much earlier when they adopt particular attitudes towards different subject areas. At a very obvious level, pupils need to know what kind of careers to aim for. This knowledge has, however, several components: (i) a balanced understanding of their own talents, potentialities, attitudes, likings, interests (but such self-knowledge is hard to come by; 'know thyself' is a central aim of the entire curriculum and it would give a distorted picture of what education was about if this became parcelled off to yet another 'expert', possibly in the person of the careers teacher); (ii) an understanding of the jobs which will satisfy those career aspirations – the conditions of work, the career prospects, the qualifications needed; (iii) acquaintance with the different educational routes to these jobs, the training programmes available, and indeed the more open-ended educational routes which are not aimed at specific jobs.

The information required by a teacher in order to give proper advice is enormous and yet changing rapidly. Anyone who feels in command of the scene in 1983 will be out of date in 1984. Indeed, I have rarely met a teacher during the in-service courses I have recently been directing who understands the complexities of BTEC or the range of training possibilities available under the New Training Initiative's Youth Training Scheme. And how could they? Without systematic in-service training, it is impossible for teachers to keep abreast of these changes.

The problem, however, goes beyond that of mastering information. There is an important educational task in coming to understand these developments and in giving the right advice to pupils. Furthermore, the right advice might go against the interests of the school. For example, the Youth Training Scheme can be seen cynically as a way of taking otherwise unemployed youngsters off the street. But it could be viewed more positively as part of a national scheme for providing continued training to all youngsters up to seventeen (and eventually eighteen) both for their personal benefit and for the benefit of the economy which requires a better skilled work force. Not only will trainees be paid an allowance but they will be better placed and better equipped to secure jobs at seventeen or eighteen than those who remain in full-time education. This wider political understanding of developments must enter into the schools' advice to young people, even though it might be in the self-interest of each school to preserve as many in the sixth form as possible.

At the same time the possibility of unemployment or of intermittent employment must be faced honestly (see Watts, 1978, for example). No longer can the carrot of a better job be the motive for working harder. I have even heard a ten-year-old expressing concern because she did not feel she would be clever enough to compete eventually for the limited number of jobs available. And certainly in secondary schools the uncertain future has entered into the consciousness of young people – not necessarily as a spur to compete more rigorously for the limited number of places but as an occasion for apathy and indeed alienation. Preparation for adult life must also be a preparation for such an uncertain future, where self-respect and status do not depend upon having a job. This, of course, raises much wider social values than the school can take on responsibility for, but the school needs to make its own educational contribution by: (i) creating a realistic awareness of the situation; (ii) enabling young people to appreciate the wider social implications of it; (iii) promoting the personal strength to be able to cope psychologically with its consequences; (iv) creating the political involvement in, rather than alienation from, a community that at the moment is prepared to tolerate such an unequal distribution of opportunities in life. These are large issues for a school to take on, and yet self-knowledge, social awareness, and political know-how could (and should) arise from the different areas of the curriculum as these have been mapped out and illustrated in chapters 5 and 6.

None the less, there is still a need for some direct focus upon careers and jobs both in class and at the level of personal guidance. And indeed programmes have been developed for systematic 'careers education'. Particular attention should be paid, for example, to the Schools Council Project *Careers Education and Guidance*, established in 1971, which has produced classroom materials and teacher guides for teaching thirteen- to eighteen-year-olds, and the work of CRAC (Careers Research and Advisory Centre) and NICEC (National Institute for Careers Education and Counselling) which have produced a range of material.[2]

Such a direct approach to preparation for employment, however, should keep in mind some important distinctions, for without these one will see once again a specific part of the timetable taking on educational tasks which belong to the curriculum as a whole or to other, more traditional, areas. These distinctions are between:

(i)   *information* about job, career, training, and educational possibilities;
(ii) *understanding the implications* of making particular choices;
(iii) *the experiences* relevant to making those choices;
(iv) *social and political awareness* of the context in which certain kinds of education, training, and jobs are available;
(v)   *the personal knowledge* (talents, interests, aptitudes and so on) relevant to making choices.

With reference to (i), there is a need certainly for an up-to-date and well-documented information service with someone who knows the material and can provide well-informed advice to enquirers, whether these be pupils or teachers who, knowing individual pupils well (but not the variety of career prospects), are seeking to guide the pupils towards appropriate courses.

With reference to (ii), there is a need for teaching and thus some place on the timetable of the fourth or fifth year. Indeed this would sensibly be combined with instruction in the kind of information suggested in (i) and in how to find one's way around the mass of information that is now accumulating in each school. There is need for some 'mapping of the territory', getting across, for example, the types and levels of training courses available in further education.

With reference to (iii), some form of work experience should be provided for all youngsters in their fifth year. There are difficulties in providing this before the fifth year, and these difficulties will increase as time goes on because work experience for trainees under the expanding YTS, combined with fewer businesses in a position to provide places, will decimate opportunities for many at school who would otherwise be able to benefit. Work experience, however, so often lacks educational value for two reasons. First, without systematic reflection it becomes a vicarious experience from which few lessons are learnt. To learn from experience is, as we know too well, a considerable achievement. Foreign travel so often is not education; without knowing how to look or what to look for, opportunities are missed. Geoff Stanton provides a useful model for experiential learning in *Experience, Reflection, Learning* (see FEU, 1978, pages 20–27); although written with Unified Vocational Programmes in mind, the model could be applied with adaptation to experiential learning in schools, in particular to learning from work experience.

This model suggests simply that the learning process should be considered as being in three phases:

> The individual's experience needs to be followed by some organised reflection. This reflection enables the individual to learn from his experience, but also helps to identify any need for some specific learning before further experience is acquired.

(page 21)

Too often the young person, having completed some work experience, is slotted back into a timetable where there is no room either for the reflective learning needed or for identifying the new skills and concepts required for getting more out of subsequent experience. Or again the very considerable experience gained by many young people from part-time work receives no acknowledgment in the schools.

A second and connected reason for work experience being non-educational is the non-developmental nature of it. Too often it is planned without reference to the previous experience the pupil has had or to what subsequently, under YTS for example, he or she may be doing. The absence of co-ordinated planning can so easily lead to a mere repetition of what previously has been experienced.

With reference to (iv) social and political awareness, this would be an integral part of the pupils' wider social education and might reasonably be expected to develop through the social studies curriculum of the school. But where a school is trying to achieve a cross-curriculum policy for personal and social education, then whoever co-ordinates it, or more particularly co-ordinates careers education, would need to ensure that development is taking place.

With reference to (v) personal knowledge, we are raising wider educational problems than can be confined to careers education, namely, what has been referred to as the 'pastoral curriculum' (see Marland, 1980).

(iii) Pastoral Curriculum

The argument is that although, as I have argued in this book, many of the 'pastoral responsibilities' are fulfilled through the general care and respect for pupils throughout the curriculum and through what is learnt in specific curriculum areas, none the less

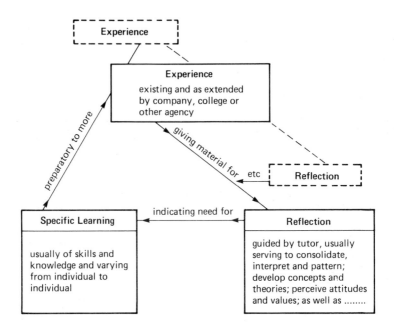

This model is not meant to describe an 'ideal format' — though it might be possible to devise a scheme by using it, or to analyse an existing one.

Thus it does not follow that the three activities or phases outlined should necessarily become separate sequential elements in a scheme. All three elements might well be present in one 'session'.

Each of the activities could take place in a variety of contexts — at work, in college, in a youth centre, for instance.

To some extent the process may occur naturally outside the curriculum, in the sense that it is not planned or facilitated by scheme organisers.

Reproduced by kind permission of the Further Education Curriculum Review and Development Unit, from page 20 of G. Stanton's *Experience, Reflection, Learning* (April, 1978).

there are certain aspects of personal growth that require systematic teaching. McLaughlin (1983, page 95) refers to those principles that

> . . . can be invoked to determine the particular problems, decisions, and adjustments facing the individual . . .

in the absence of which there are likely to be the crises for which individual and *ad hoc* pastoral care will be required. McLaughlin suggests four conditions which such a curriculum programme will need to satisfy:

   (i)   it will equip the young person to deal with a range of problems, decisions, and adjustments that are likely to confront any person in our society;
  (ii)   the ability to deal with such 'problems, decisions, and adjustments' is not likely to be brought about by other means;
 (iii)   the school has the relevant expertise;
  (iv)   such a programme should not get in the way of the primary task of the school, namely, a liberal education.

These conditions – apart from (iv) – seem eminently sensible, and they serve as a warning to schools that either embark on activities for which they are not equipped or (as in the case of health education) encroach upon issues that are better dealt with in other areas of the curriculum such as the humanities or social studies.

Marland (1980) provides some substance to such a curriculum. It has three parts – the educational, the vocational, and the personal. Here I am concerned mainly with the 'personal'. This would include (Marland, page 162):

   (i)   self-knowledge;
  (ii)   understanding of and coping with physical and emotional well-being;
 (iii)   interpersonal relationships and skills;
  (iv)   rights and obligations;
   (v)   choosing and decision-making;
  (vi)   utilising public facilities and services;
 (vii)   significant social conventions;
(viii)   seeing things from others' point of view;
  (ix)   using time significantly – hobbies, and so on.

Such a programme would doubtless be the place where the

relevance of literature and work within the humanities is brought into focus upon the 'problems, decisions, and adjustments' that any person might be expected to deal with – and do so through the experiences recounted by the members of the class. It would also be the place where the personal guidance and counselling that must go side by side with careers information might begin. What, in effect, is being said is that there is a need for a more skilled and systematic approach to the role of personal tutor and to the period set aside for this work.

Indeed, in this lies the significance of Leslie Button's work and of that of Baldwin and Wells (1979, 1980, 1981) who have expanded Button's developmental group work in a particular direction. Button (1974 and 1980) argues that the peer group is of crucial importance in socialising the child and in either enhancing or stunting the child's personal growth; that the teacher needs to work more directly through normal group interactions and sensitivities; that this can be approached systematically as part of the curriculum of the school; and that with proper training teachers can acquire the skills for such developmental group work. Indeed, in his later work, Button (1981, 1982) provides a course of learning activities. These are developmental, not in the strong sense explained in chapter 3, but in the sense of a gradual acquisition of skills and sensitivities where the earlier ones are presupposed by the later ones. According to Button (1980, page 71):

> A very different kind of programme (from a mainly cognitive one) is required in order to help young people in their social skills and self-feelings. The young person must himself be the focus of the exchange. And a step-by-step exploration will be needed, where each step enables the young person to cope with the next deeper step. The programme would proceed from a study of the situation in which they find themselves, to an examination of their own attitudes and behaviour, to their manner and skills in coping with other people – friends, peers in general, the opposite sex, their parents and siblings, with strangers, adults, and people in authority – and from there to the deeper self-feelings that influence every department of life so strongly.

What therefore is distinctive about Button's work is the active and experiential learning model – not just for the pupils but initially for the teachers who will be teaching it (see, for example, Stoate's 1983 account of a training programme in action).

The most obvious place for developmental group work as the central core of the 'pastoral curriculum' is the tutorial period, although the teaching strategies and general orientation could with profit be extended into differrent curriculum areas. The teacher tutor is one who has responsibility for the personal welfare of a group of pupils, but too often feels lacking in those skills that a personal tutor needs. Individual guidance and counselling are therefore often referred to a professional counsellor. But guidance and counselling should be seen as an integral part of the educational provision of young people, and it is interesting to note that this is acknowledged by MSC requirements for YTS (see MSC, 1981) and by FEU in its blueprint of pre-vocational courses (see FEU, 1979). As an integral part, they fall naturally within the 'pastoral curriculum' as I have briefly described it rather than become the prerogative of the professional counsellor or trouble-shooter within the school. Teachers may, of course, flee from such responsibilities because little in their training has equipped them for them. But as guidance and counselling become more widely acknowledged as an integral, rather than exceptional, part of the educational process, so the teaching skills are identified more explicitly and in-service programmes made available.[3]

The main lesson of these examples, however briefly referred to, is to show that there is already extant enough curriculum development and knowledge about teaching skills for a school to draw upon in developing a 'pastoral curriculum' and vocational guidance as part of its overall programme of personal and social education. The one thing necessary for success, however, is the in-service training of teachers in the skills and strategies which shift the approach from instruction to facilitating the active and experiential learning that is at the centre of Button's and Miller's work (see FEU, 1982a).

2 Recording, Assessing, Profiling

'Recording' is simply making a note or giving a description of what has happened without attempting to evaluate it. 'Assessing' entails some form of measurement – seeing a performance against certain standards which may or may not be clearly defined. To note that a girl has helped another child is to record a fact; to say that she thereby accomplished a task set her or to say that she is therefore a good pupil is to assess her. One very important distinction implicit in the two kinds of assessment I have just given is that between criterion-referenced and norm-referenced assessments. To say that she has accomplished a task is to say that her performance comes up to certain standards, meets certain criteria which have been established beforehand. To say that she is a good girl is, generally speaking, to make implicit comparisons with other pupils, to place her in a continuum somewhere between the out-and-out wicked and the excellent.

When the Assessment of Performance Unit established a working party to explore the possibility of monitoring pupil performance within the area of personal and social development, it met with considerable opposition from within the consultative committee. Eventually it was decided not to proceed. The arguments against monitoring performance in this area were as follows. To monitor performance you would need, first, to record what pupils actually do and, secondly, to engage in some form of assessment. However, such an exercise could be objected to along the following lines:

(i)   *philosophical*: even recording requires the selection of behaviours as significant from the personal, social and moral point of view and assessing implies there are standards of acceptable behaviour; however, this is an area where there are no objective standards on the basis of which one can either select or assess.

(ii) *moral*: recording and assessing in this area will involve an undesirable encroachment upon privacy and the rights of the individual.

(iii) *political*: the collection of knowledge in this area has potential dangers since it might give information about personal behaviour, which is of a private nature, to a public body.

(iv) *technical*: whereas in maths, science, and language there are techniques available for assessing development, there are no such techniques in personal and social education and, moreover, the territory is too vast and amorphous for any useful developments to take place.

These were objections levelled against monitoring at the national level, but, if valid, they apply equally to recording and assessing at local, school, and classroom levels. In the light of what has been argued in this book, how valid are these objections?

First, there is something paradoxical in holding the view that personal, social and moral development is the most important aspect of education whilst at the same time arguing that there are no criteria either for selecting what is significant in this development or for assessing what counts as having developed successfully. If there are no such criteria, then anything counts as development and there is no point in teaching or fostering one kind of development rather than another. Of course, the argument is difficult, and there will be no argument which will not have its critics. But objectivity does not depend in this or in any other area (language, mathematical, or scientific) upon universal agreement. It is a contradiction to say that personal development is important, whilst at the same time arguing that there are no criteria implicit within the public form of discourse that we, as teachers, participate in for assessing that development. That is why it was so important in the first half of this book to explore philosophically what it means to be a person and to develop as a person, and what it means to be moral and to develop morally. My argument may be wrong in parts, but at least it is stated objectively so that others, in reading it, can point out the errors and lead me and others to a more defensible way of describing personal, social and moral development. With such a philosophical foundation, one can more confidently select those aspects of being a person and of personal development which can be the basis of a monitoring programme.

Secondly, the identification of personal and moral development with what are essentially matters of private concern is to neglect the wider social significance of personal knowledge, attitudes, and behaviour. This objection is indeed the product of an individualism (stress on autonomy) which fails to see the wider social responsibilities of individuals or indeed the inseparable links between individual development and development within a community. Indeed, as I have stressed throughout the book and as is emphasised so well by Dewey, the links are essentially dynamic and reciprocal. The kind of community we all share in depends upon the sort of individual that develops (as Devlin, 1965, pointed out there is no area of private morality which does not in some way affect public morality), and in turn the morality of the community will affect the morality of the individual (hence, the importance for Kohlberg of creating 'a just community' and for Power and Reimer of creating the appropriate 'classroom atmosphere'). If we want to live in a just society, then it is important to take note of and to do something about the just or unjust behaviour of young people.

Thirdly, similar points can be made from the political angle. Certainly, one has no right in a society, which still values freedom of opinion and of expression, to probe the specific political views of individuals, or indeed to use one's authority as a teacher to change these. But the ability (the concepts, skills, and practical knowledge) to participate politically in a democracy is of concern to those who wish to see a free and democratic society preserved. To promote such abilities, however, requires some assessment by the teacher of where the pupils are at, and the political knowledge and know-how that they have.

Finally, we have seen in this book various techniques for establishing the level of moral and social reasoning that pupils are capable of. The Assessment of Performance Unit supported a comprehensive review of the literature about existing assessment techniques in personal and social development (see Schofield, 1981) and this provides a useful source of information for researchers and others. But this is a difficult territory to get to grips with – there are pupil behaviour inventories, techniques for measuring social sensitivities (see Light, 1980), attitude assessments (see Mathews, 1974), the effective domain (see Krathwohl et al., 1964), and of course innumerable ways of discovering the kind of knowledge concepts that young people possess. One needs to preserve a certain common-sense attitude towards all this literature. Assessment is a matter of making judgments and teachers are necessarily making them all the time without the help of sophisticated techniques. What is necessary is a greater degree of objectivity than is often the case but 'objectivity' requires, firstly, that the basis of one's judgments is made explicit and public and is defended when challenged by colleagues or others; and, secondly, that the judgments themselves are open to scrutiny of others.

None the less, there are dangers in assessment. The boundaries between private territory and public rights, between personal taste and educational responsibility, between individual autonomy and community interest, are by no means clear cut, and, unless one is constantly on one's guard, there is always the danger of personal values being encroached upon by the over-zealous (or the power seeking) public officer. For that reason we need to remind ourselves of the different purposes of recording and assessing.

(i) National and Local Monitoring

Those who are responsible for running the educational system and those who pay their taxes towards it will want to know whether the system is functioning well, or whether more money, research, or effort needs to be put into certain sections which are not functioning as well as they should be. In so far as personal and social education is seen to be an important aim of education, it is reasonable for politicians, administrators, and the public to know whether that aim is being fulfilled. Indeed, not to monitor in this area (as the APU have decided) could so easily give the impression that, despite the claims to the contrary, this is not an important area when compared with mathematics or science.

Monitoring, however, for this purpose does not require knowledge about individual pupils or indeed schools. How this might be achieved is open to debate, but an example is available in the monitoring exercise of NAEP (National Assessment of Educational Progress), which has a rolling programme of monitoring pupil performance across the USA in ten subject areas. Two areas – social studies and civics – are relevant. There have been three NAEP surveys in the areas of citizenship and social studies, in 1969–72, 1973–74, and finally 1981–82. The last survey amalgamated the two areas into one because of the similarity between the goals which were considered to be important in citizenship and social studies. The results of this survey are not yet available.

Both citizenship and social studies were defined by the list of major objectives which it was agreed (amongst teachers, academics, and representatives of the community) should be tested under these labels. The following illustration of the use of objectives for monitoring purposes is taken from the second survey on citizenship.

What gives coherence to the different objectives is the underlying concern for maintaining a democratic form of life. 'As a government of the people, by the people, for the people, it is implicit that our nation depends upon the participation of an educated and informed public in order to survive and prosper.'

The seven major objectives to be tested were:

I   *Show Concern for the Well-Being and Dignity of Others*
   A   Treat others with respect.
   B   Consider the consequences for others of their own actions.
   C   Guard safety and health of others.

D   Offer help to others in need.
E   Support equal opportunity in education, housing, employment and recreation.
F   Are loyal to country, to friends, and to other groups whose values they share.
G   Are ethical and dependable in work, school, and social situations.

II   *Support Just Law and the Rights of All Individuals*
A   Understand the need for law.
B   Recognise specific constitutional rights and liberties.
C   Defend rights and liberties of all kinds of people.
D   Encourage ethical and lawful behaviour in others.
E   Comply with public laws.
F   Oppose unjust rules, laws, and authority by lawful means.

III   *Know the Main Structure and Functions of Their Governments*
A   Recognise basic governmental purposes.
B   Understand the organisation of federal and state governments.
C   Know the political structure of their local community.
D   Recognise the relationships of different levels of government.
E   Recognise the importance of political opposition and interest groups.
F   Recognise that democracy depends on the alertness and involvement of its citizens, and know how citizens can affect government.
G   Know structure of school and student government.

IV   *Participate in Democratic Civic Improvement*
A   Believe that each person's civic behaviour is important, and convey this belief to others.
B   Favour organised civic action where it is needed.
C   Actively work for civic improvement.
D   Participate in local, state, and national governmental processes.
E   Apply democratic procedures effectively in small groups.

V   *Understand Important World, National, and Local Civic Problems*
A   Understand social conflict among individuals, groups,

and nations and the difficulties in achieving peace and social harmony.

B   Recognise how different civic policies may affect people's efforts to meet their economic needs.

C   Recognise major environmental problems and are aware of alternative civic solutions.

D   See relations among civic problems and particular events.

E   Generate good ideas about causes and solutions for civic problems.

VI   *Approach Civic Decisions Rationally*
   A   Seek relevant information and alternative viewpoints on civicly important decisions.
   B   Evaluate civic communications and actions carefully as a basis for forming and changing their own views.
   C   Plan and organise civic tasks effectively.
   D   Support open, honest communication and universal education.

VII   *Help and Respect their own Families*
   A   Co-operate in home responsibilities and help provide for other family members.
   B   Instill civic values and skills in other family members.

It should be noted that, as in the statement of objectives for all NAEP assessment, these objectives need to be related to the particular age group being assessed. For example: 'Guard safety and health of others.' (*I*, C above.)

Age 9   They report physical hazards, such as broken electrical wires, faulty equipment, and fire hazards. They know fire escape and water rescue procedures. They properly dispose of containers of medicines, cleansers, poisons, and other potentially dangerous products. They know how cleanliness may prevent the spread of germs; they know first aid practices and how to get emergency medical help. They set examples of safety at school and on the streets.

Age 13   (In addition to Age 9)
   They know how contagious diseases are spread and take preventive action, such as covering garbage or staying home when sick. They caution peers on the dangers of drugs, tobacco, and alcohol.

Age 17   (In addition to Ages 9 and 13)
They instruct others in safety practices and set examples of safety at work and recreation. They drive carefully and avoid driving while under the influence of alcohol or drugs or when very ill or upset. They support efforts by private groups and government to promote public health, such as water safety and first aid courses, safer automobiles, regulation and labelling of drugs, and pollution control.

Adult   (In addition to Ages 9, 13, and 17)
If their property is used by others (for example, apartments, offices, playgrounds) they keep it in safe and healthful condition. They comply with safety and health rules at work and in the community. They know how to turn on and off gas and electricity where they live in case of fire, flood, or other emergency and know procedures to follow in case of a major disaster.

It is argued by NAEP, as it is by APU, that assessment aims to monitor what is being taught in school. It does not try to determine what should be taught. However, the very mapping out of citizenship – the establishment of categories through which data can be selected and processed – defines citizenship in a particular way, puts a value on certain qualities rather than others, and thus sets standards of what a citizenship course should strive for.

Having decided upon the objectives in some detail, exercises and items are written for measuring these items. The items need to conform to a very strict formula (see Pring, 1982, page 18).[4] The following is an example of an item considered for the citizenship/social studies third cycle of assessment.

Main Objective IV   The ways human beings organise, adapt to and change their environment.

Sub Objective B
Including 3   The organisation of human societies, understanding how family, economic, political, religious and educational structures differ (for example, nuclear and extended families; barter and monetary economies; authoritarian and democratic governments; monotheistic and polytheistic religion; formal and informal learning).

Item   In the United States, people spend a considerable part of their incomes on buying all sorts of insurance. In traditional China, there are no insurance companies. It is reasonable to assume which one of the following about traditional China?

1 There were no accidents or misfortunes in Chinese life.
2 The Chinese were able to bear any hardship without provision for security.
3 Something in Chinese life took the place of insurance.
4 Life was very cheap in traditional China.
5 I don't know.

Item Documentation

Item Number: 1065
Short Text: Insurance in China
Objective Identifier: IV B 3
Matrix Identifier: I A L

Content Rationale: Because structures differ from culture to culture, we often assume that our culture makes sense, another doesn't. This item uses insurance as a case in point. To arrive at the correct foil students have to assume that the Chinese were human beings and had a cultural equivalent for insurance. Such understanding is vital as a social value.

Foil Rationales: Correct foil is number 3. To arrive at this answer, one has to assume that the Chinese were human and that there was an equivalent to insurance in Chinese culture. In fact, families took immediate responsibility for any misfortunes and acted as 'insurance companies' to absorb losses and provide for people. However, one does not have to know this particular fact to correctly answer the item.

Incorrect foils: Foil number 1 is incorrect, because the Chinese were human and did have accidents. Foil number 2 is incorrect: this is a stereotype and a good distractor foil for students who fall prey to stereotypes. Foil number 4 is incorrect: again, this is a stereotype.

Age Appropriateness and Difficulty: 9-E-M-D 13-E-M-D 17-E-M-D

After the tests, the following are published:

(i)   the detailed objectives of the tests;
(ii)   an overview, presenting the results of the assessment;
(iii) demonstration packages of items;
(iv)   a comparison between the results of this and previous cycles of tests.

The importance of NAEP is that it is the most thorough attempt yet to establish national monitoring of pupil performance across the curriculum, including areas of personal and social development. In a recent paper (Pring, 1982) I have set out the objectives, shown in detail the processes that NAEP went through to arrive at these objectives and subsequent test items, looked critically at these, and suggested lessons that might be learnt from the NAEP's work.

(ii)   Monitoring a School

Schools are increasingly vulnerable to quick evaluation and rash judgments from the public as numbers fall and parental choice increases. Schools have to give an account of themselves to outsiders. Too often these accounts refer only to academic achievements as these are measured by public examination results. And yet what a school is achieving in personal and social education is of more importance if the argument of this book is correct. How can a school display its achievements in this area? There is always the danger of sounding too pretentious, or of falling into the rhetoric of self-praise which impresses very few. First, a school would need to take personal and social education sufficiently seriously to say in detail what it is trying to achieve and to show why, in the light of the evidence, it thinks it is achieving it. This does require some careful mapping of the territory and taking the public, especially the parents, into its confidence in developing its programme. There is evidence to show that parents are as much concerned with the personal welfare and development of their pupils as they are with academic results (see Elliott, 1981) and that personal qualities and attitudes are as important to employers as the 'basic skills'.

There are ways for professionals within the school to examine more objectively the atmosphere and the hidden values which

affect their professional work. Rutter *et al.* (1979) demonstrated
one way. But the most important step for a school in examining its
own performance is to get the questions right. On pages 30 and 110
I have suggested questions which the staff as a whole might profit
from considering. On page 114 I have suggested a matrix which
would enable the staff to look at the different aspects and to match
them up with different curriculum areas. This at least would be the
beginning of a self-monitoring exercise, but it would require, too,
some kind of action research – the gathering of evidence and of
different perspectives – into what in practice was happening.

(iii)   Monitoring Pupil Performance

The critics of recording and assessing in this area are quite rightly
apprehensive of rash judgments being made which affect others'
attitudes towards the children and which, by being placed on
records, achieve a degree of permanancy which they do not
warrant.

Various distinctions are required here. First, there is the distinction between those aspects which are concerned with the
development of knowledge and understanding (for example, the
mastery of key political concepts) and those which are more
closely related to attitudes and values. Learning difficulties di-
agnosed in the former are as important to record as those in
mathematics or science. The latter, however, are much less easy to
specify with confidence and are more likely, too, to affect others'
attitudes towards the pupils.

Secondly, there is the distinction between records and assessment, which are the property of those in authority, and those
which are the property of the young persons themselves. A
significant contribution to this area has been made by Don
Stansbury whose Record of Personal Achievement (RPA) (now
known as the Swindon Scheme) and his (later) Record of Personal
Experience (RPE) suggest ways in which the pupil can, as part of
the curriculum, be actively involved in recording what he or she
sees from a personal point of view to be important achievements.

RPA has been described as 'a system based on the idea of a
personally compiled pupil record, which seeks to encourage and
reward personal qualities commonly considered to form an
important aim of education' (Swales, 1979, page 7). It achieved
this aim by providing pupils with loose-leaf record books in which
a personal curriculum vitae could be written during the final two

years at school. The way the record was to be kept was structured so that personal qualities and achievements would be publicised. Stansbury has built upon the RPA experience in developing his more recent RPE work at Kings School, Totnes.[5]

The main disappointment with RPA and RPE is that in practice it has been used almost exclusively by the low-achieving fourth and fifth year pupils, although the principles are equally valid for the whole range of ability.

Innovations within the area do, however, so often occur with the less academic pupils. One reason for this is that, in failing to show academic achievement as judged by examination results, they would otherwise have no record of what they have achieved as a result of eleven years of compulsory schooling. And yet so often they have achieved a great deal: first, in mastering a range of knowledge, skills, concepts, practical know-how which, however, may not be what is needed to pass public examinations; secondly, in developing personal qualities, a sense of responsibility, social skills, a mature outlook on life, all of which are not (quite rightly) tapped by public examinations. There has, therefore, been a growth of interest in pupil profiles which would give a more generous picture of personal achievement and development than is possible in a certificate of public examination passes.[6]

This is much too big a topic to go into here in any detail. FEU's (1982b) 'review of issues and practice in the use and development of student profiles' is a useful summary of 'the state of the art'. There have been four major developments. There are the two Schools Council Projects – one for England reported by Balogh (1982), one for Wales. Thirdly, there are initial trial profiles of the FEU (1982b) which have been adapted for CGLI Vocational Preparation (General) Courses. Fourthly, there is the pioneering work of the 'Scottish Pupil Profile System' (see Broadfoot, 1980).

Pratley (1982) summarises the purpose of profiles:

(i)   provide an alternative means of recording attainment . . . and in most cases provide supplementary information about a student's experiences and performance. In this respect they are a summative record, available for the student to take away, and use as evidence of attainment in progressing to other courses or jobs;

(ii) provide a record of what has been achieved at any point within a course . . . In this respect they are a formative record . . .

(iii)   provide a guide to what still needs to be learned . . . The curriculum is therefore made explicit to the learner, and in this respect the profile acts as a focus for the negotiation of learning agendas;

(iv)   provide a focus for the guidance and counselling . . . The discussions between teacher and learner that need to take place in the compilation of profile records are likely to lead to an improved understanding by the learner of his/her needs and possible future directions;

(v)   provide the motivation and continuous feedback on progress which is a feature of any good scheme of continuous assessment.

Most examples of profiles have pre-vocational or vocational students in mind. They have one eye on future employers and parts of the profiles are open to criticism in stressing basic skills as these are spelt out in rather specific behaviours. But this need not be the case, and schools and groups of schools (for example, Teignmouth School, South Devon and the Exeter Scheme; see also Fletcher, 1980, on 'The Sutton Centre Profile') adapted the profiles profitably for their own purposes.

This, of course, is more relevant to secondary than to primary schools. But profiles are but ways of recording pupils' achievements, and keeping records is as much the responsibility of primary as it is of secondary schools. Fletcher (1980) gives a valuable account of record keeping in primary schools. Devon local authority (1978) has produced guidelines for schools for keeping records of pupils from five to sixteen which stress the importance of personal and social qualities and interests. Again, however, all this can distract the individual teacher or school from sorting out what it means by personal and social education, mapping out the territory, establishing a cross-curriculum policy, determining the different objectives that might be achieved either through the curriculum as a whole or through distinct parts of it, and then in the light of this deciding what needs to be recorded. Two key questions then arise: first, how should this recording and assessment be achieved; secondly, what degree of privacy (from children or parents) and of permanency should be given to such records.

One can worry too much about these questions. Once you have established what is to be achieved under personal, social and moral education the ways of recording and assessing (sufficient for helping one with the task of teaching) will no doubt suggest themselves. And on the whole one should err on the side of temporary records. Their main purpose after all is to help with the task of teaching.

NOTES

1   *Pastoral Care in Education*, Oxford: Basil Blackwell, which was first published in February 1983.
2   Three organisations can provide valuable information, advice, and literature on careers and vocational guidance. They are:
   (i)   CRAC (Careers Research and Advisory Centre), Bateman Street, Cambridge;
   (ii) NICEC (National Institute for Careers Education and Counselling), Bayfordbury House, Lower Hatfield, Hertford;
   (iii) Counselling and Career Development Unit, University of Leeds, Leeds, LS2 9JT.
   (iv) Schools Council Project *Careers Education and Guidance* pupil and teacher material entitled *Work* published by Longman, Harlow, Essex.

CRAC has produced a practical 'Your Choice' series which gives advice to parents, teachers, and students on choices which face students at 13+, 15+, and 17+. (See March and Smith, 1977; Smith and Matthews, 1980; Smith and March, 1981.) Because the scene is changing rapidly, these books are constantly being brought up to date.

On approaches to occupational choice, self and occupational awareness, career patterns, assessment, and so on, with implications for practice, a useful collection of papers is Watts, Super and Kidd (1981). Useful articles by the director of CRAC are Watts (1978) 'The implications of school leaver unemployment for careers education in schools' and (1980) 'Pastoral care and careers education'. Despite its being seven years old, Law and Watts (1977), which is a study of some approaches to careers education in schools, is still of value to the careers teacher.

Careers or vocational guidance is increasingly seen to be part of wider personal guidance. There has been an interesting set of publications in recent years on social and life skills. The connection between vocational and personal and life skills is seen particularly in John Miller's *Tutoring* (see FEU, 1982a), which offers practical guidance and counselling help to the tutor in vocational preparation; in Hayes and Hopson (1971), which links proper careers guidance with psychological testing and the development of self-concept and self-assessment; and in Hopson and Hough (1973), which provides exercises in personal development prior to exercises in careers development.

A pioneering book that has proved its worth over the years is Howden and Dowson (1973), which argued for vocational guidance to be an integral part of the curriculum.

Computers have come to the aid of careers teachers through the JIIG/CAL Project (Job Ideas and Information Generator/Computer Assisted Learning), and you can read about it in Closs and Broderick (1982).

3   There has been a considerable growth of literature, with practical guidance, under the general title of social and life skills. Although very useful, with a firm theoretical foundation, they need to be approached critically since there is a danger of seeing success in living to be essentially a matter of acquiring a set of teachable skills. In particular, one might find useful Hopson and Scally (1981) *Lifeskills Teaching* (and make use of the teaching programmes, Hopson and Scally (1979) Numbers 1 and 2); Hargie, Saunders and Dickson (1981) *Social Skills in Interpersonal Communication*; Ellis and Whittington (1981) *A Guide to Social Skill Training*; Light (1980) *The Development of Social Sensitivity*; and Wilkinson and Canter (1982) *Social Skills Training Manual*. For work with mentally handicapped students a useful book is Whelan and Speake (1979) *Learning to Cope*.

Other valuable books on pastoral care that are not so narrowly 'skills based' but provide practical guidance are by Marland (1974) *Pastoral Care*; Hamblin (1974) *The Teacher and Counselling*; Hamblin (1978) *The Teacher and Pastoral Care*; and Blackburn (1975) *The Tutor*.

4   A copy of my paper 'National assessment of social studies' is obtainable from Professor R. A. Pring, University of Exeter School of Education, St Lukes, Heavitree Road, Exeter.

5   Details of RPE (Record of Personal Experience) can be found in Don Stansbury's own accounts: 'The record of personal experience' (1980) and *Record of Personal Experience, Qualities and Qualifications* (1976). The system has been adopted in many schools throughout the country, and Don Stansbury is now able to work part-time upon improving the system and helping other schools to develop it. Address: Kings School, Totnes, Devon.

6   Teachers often believe that employers are only interested in examination results. But this is belied by what little research there is. Employers are as interested in personal and social qualities and indeed, apart from the 'high level' jobs that require specific qualifications, do not seem too concerned about the details of the diplomas or certificates that the employees or applicants have. Obviously the qualification and the degree of importance attached to them depend on the kind of job (the technical complexity, and so on) that we are

talking about. One valuable research study in this respect, which is still unpublished, is that of Jones (1983), 'The uses employers make of examination results and other tests for selection and employment'. This has implications for the planning of profiles. One of the most disturbing aspects of this report was the ignorance of employers about the significance of grades in CSE or GCE examinations and the apparent lack of concern (with some notable exceptions) amongst employers, examination boards, and schools about overcoming that ignorance.

Conclusion

The headmaster quoted in the introduction was, quite understandably, suspicious of education. He had witnessed what learned engineers, educated physicians, trained nurses, and college graduates can do. His request therefore to those who teach was brief: help your students become human.

One might anticipate two quite opposite reactions to such a request. First, it assumes a knowledge, an expertise, and indeed a touch of moral superiority which none of us can claim and for which no one can be trained. There are experts in mathematics and in physics, in history and in geography – but in being human? Secondly, one might act with enthusiasm. Making people human is taken as the central educational task. Programmes of personal and social education are created, published, and added to the already crowded curriculum. But more often than not the sheer complexity and size of the task leads to insuperable problems in translating aims into practice.

This book aims to show that conceptual sense can be made of personal and social education as a curriculum aim and that broad aims can be translated into practical terms, just as in any other area of the curriculum. It does indeed need detailed and systematic analysis of what one is aiming at. But this can be pursued without any implication of moral superiority. Rather does it require a careful, philosophical reflection upon what it means to be a person, how development as a person is inextricably linked with a form of social life, and where moral values and ideas are presupposed in both. And this philosophical reflection should be part of the professional job of those who introduce personal and social education into the curriculum and into the life of the school.

This book aims to help teachers with their deliberation, not to be a substitute for it. At the same time it points to the theoretical work which might be linked with such an analysis and which provides a firmer bases for practical developments. What, then, might we tentatively conclude?

1   Although there are elements within the content of timetabled subjects which make a valuable contribution to personal development, it would be wrong to identify personal and social education with any subject, new or old. Indeed that would divert attention from the most important questions that a school needs to ask about its impact upon the personal development of young people.

2   A school, therefore, should start by examining the effect of the school and the curriculum as a whole upon young persons – upon their sense of personal worth, upon their self-confidence and sense of achievement, upon the relationships of trust and co-operation between teacher and pupil and between pupil and pupil. This, of course, requires close attention to what we mean by respecting them as persons. At the end of chapter 2, I suggest the kind of questions schools should, in the light of the foregoing analysis, be asking about how they help or hinder pupils in their development of respect for themselves and in their acceptance of responsibility for their own deeds and decisions.

3   There is, however, a developmental aspect to this growth as a person – a slow but definite change in the quality of how young people see things from another's point of view, how they reason about matters of moral concern, how they understand and operate within a system of rules, and how they acquire the personal strength and independence to withstand outer pressures and inner wayward feelings.

4   We need, therefore, to attend in particular to the social and institutional setting which enhances or discourages these various lines of development. What is overwhelmingly evident is that the key to this development lies in the way in which authority is understood and exercised by those in positions of power. For Piaget the shift had to be made from unilateral respect for those in authority to mutual respect; but that could be achieved only if those exercising authority did so in an appropriate manner – respecting, as potentially autonomous persons, those in their care. For Kohlberg, 'just communities' were a prerequisite for getting individual people to take seriously principles of justice in their daily behaviour.

5 We might, however, extend these more general points about institutional authority to the relationships and the ethos or atmosphere of individual classrooms – to the place of discussion in classroom learning, or to the treatment of personal difficulties, or to the respect for pupils' views. Teaching methods in any subject have their hidden values.

6 In the more specific area of moral development, there is a sufficiently firm basis in research and curriculum development for deciding how one might justify and promote relevant skills, concepts, attitudes, and habits. In particular, however, it is important that the acquisition of appropriate habits and rule-following behaviour in early childhood should be followed later by attempts to reveal the principles lying behind the specific do's and don'ts. But, again, concern for the moral behaviour of individuals requires equal concern for the moral atmosphere of the institutions to which they belong.

7 It would, however, be negligent indeed for this concern for personal, social and moral development to be so narrowly focused upon the curriculum of the school that it neglected the wider social values that are transmitted through schooling – or indeed the influence that schooling must have upon those wider social values. Personal development has its political aspect – even if confined to its development of the capacity to think, to criticise, and not to accept injustices lying down. There is a need, as I explained my conclusion to chapter 5, for teachers to be ever more vigilant of the gradual destruction, in the increasingly pragmatic and utilitarian approach to education, of those humanistic values which have, through literature and the arts, been central to our educational tradition.

8 Despite the overriding emphasis upon the values that permeate the life of the school as a whole, in particular the way in which authority is exercised, there is a need to respect, too, the need for learning specific concepts, attitudes, abilities, and habits, and the place for this will be through normal timetabled subjects. None the less, this requires, first, co-ordination of the different subject contributions and, secondly, reappraisal within the subjects of their content and method.

Bibliography

ABBS, P. (1976) *Root and Blossom*. London: Heinemann.

APPLE, M. W. (1979) *Ideology and Curriculum*. London: Routledge and Kegan Paul.

ARISTOTLE translated by Thomson, J. A. K. (1953) *The Ethics of Aristotle*, The Nichomachean Ethics. Harmondsworth, Middlesex: Penguin.

ASSESSMENT OF PERFORMANCE UNIT (1981) *Personal and Social Development*. London: DES.

AYER, A. J. (1946, 2nd ed.) *Language, Truth and Logic*. London: Gollancz.

BALDING, J. (1983) 'Developing the Health Related Behaviour Questionnaire', *Education and Health*, 1 (1).

BALDWIN, J. and WELLS, H. (eds) (1979, 1980, 1981) *Active Tutorial Work*, Books 1 to 5. Oxford: Basil Blackwell.

BALL, C. and BALL, M. (1973) *Education for a Change?* Harmondsworth: Penguin.

BALOGH, J. (1982) *Profile Reports for School Leavers*. Harlow: Longman.

BANTOCK, G. H. (1955, 2nd ed.) *Freedom and Authority in Education*. London: Faber and Faber.

BANTOCK, G. H. (1963) *Education in an Industrial Society*. London: Faber and Faber.

BANTOCK, G. H. (1965) *Education and Values: Essays in the theory of education*. London: Faber and Faber.

BANTOCK, G. H. (1967) *Education, Culture, and the Emotions*. London: Faber and Faber.

BANTOCK, G. H. (1971) 'Towards a theory of popular education', *Times Educational Supplement* 12 and 19 March, reprinted in HOOPER, R. (1971) *The Curriculum*. Edinburgh: Oliver and Boyd.

BANTOCK, G. H. (1981) *The Parochialism of the Present*. London: Routledge and Kegan Paul

BENJAMIN, H. (1971) 'The sabre-tooth curriculum', in HOOPER, R. (1971) *The Curriculum*. Edinburgh: Oliver & Boyd.

BERG, L. (1966) *Folk Tales for Reading and Telling*. Leicester: Brockhampton Press.

BLACKBURN, K. (1975) *The Tutor*. London: Heinemann Educational.

BLASI, A. (1980) 'Bridging moral cognition and moral action: a critical review of the literature', *Psychological Bulletin* 88 (1).

BLATT, H. and KOHLBERG, L. (1975) 'The effects of classroom moral discussion upon children's level of moral judgment', *Journal of Moral Education* 4.

BOWLES, S. and GINTIS, H. (1976) *Schooling in Capitalist America*. London: Routledge & Kegan Paul.

BOYD, J. (1977) *Community Education and Urban Schools*. London: Longman.

BRANDES, D. and PHILLIPS, H. (1979) *Gamester's Handbook*. London: Hutchinson.

BROADFOOT, P. (1980) 'Scottish Pupil Profile System' in BURGESS, T. and ADAMS, E. (1980) *Outcomes in Education*. London: Macmillan.

BROCKINGTON, D., WHITE, R. and PRING, R. A. (1983) *Implementing the 14 to 18 Curriculum: new approaches*. Bristol: The Youth Education Service/Bristol Social Education Project.

BRUNER, J. S. (1966) *Towards a Theory of Instruction*. Cambridge, Mass.: Harvard University Press.

BRUNER, J. (1975) 'The autogenesis of speech acts', *Journal of Child Language*, 2.

BULL, N. (1969) *Moral Education*. London: Routledge and Kegan Paul.

BUTTON, L. (1974) *Developmental Group Work with Adolescents*. London: Hodder and Stoughton.

BUTTON, L. (1980) 'The Skills of Group Tutoring' in BEST, R., JARVIS, C. and RIBBINS, P. (eds) *Perspectives in pastoral care*. London: Heinemann.

BUTTON, L. (1981, 1982) *Group Tutoring for the Form Teacher: 1 Lower Secondary School, 2 Upper Secondary School*. London: Hodder and Stoughton.

CHANDLER, E. (1980) *Educating Adolescent Girls*. London: Allen and Unwin.

CLOSS, S. J. and BRODERICK, W. R. (1982) 'Choosing careers by computer', *Education* 159 (17).

COLBY, A. *et al.* (1977) 'Secondary school moral discussion programmes led by social studies teachers', *Journal of moral education* 6.

COLBY, A. *et al.* (1983a) *The Measurement of Moral Judgment*, Vols I and II. New York: Cambridge University Press.

COLBY, A. *et al.* (1983b) *A Longitudinal Study of Moral Judgment: a monograph for the society of research in child development* Chicago, Ill.: University of Chicago Press.

COVENTRY EDUCATION COMMITTEE (1982) *Comprehensive Education for Life: A consultative document*.

COX, E. (1983) *Problems and Possibilities for Religious Education*. London: Hodder and Stoughton.

CRAFT, M. (ed.) (1982) *Teaching in a Multi-cultural Society: the task for the teacher*. London: Falmer Press.

CRICK, B. and HEATER, D. (1977) *Essays on Political Education*. London: Falmer Press.

CRICK, B. and PORTER, A. (1978) *Political Education and Political Literacy*. Harlow: Longman.

CURRICULUM REVIEW UNIT (1983) *Teaching Political Literacy*. London: Hansard Society and the University of London Institute of Education.

DAMON, W. (1977) *The Social World of the Child*. San Francisco, Calif.: Jossey-Bass.

DANCY, J. C. (1980) 'The notion of the ethos of a school', *Perspectives 1*. Exeter: University School of Education.

DEARDEN, R. F. (1972) 'Autonomy and education' in DEARDEN, R. F., HIRST, P. H. and PETERS, R. S. (eds) *Education and the Development of Reason*. London: Routledge and Kegan Paul.

DES (1977) *Education in Schools: A Consultative Document*. London: HMSO.

DES (1979) *A Framework for the School Curriculum*. London: HMSO.

DES (1981) *The School Curriculum*. London: HMSO.

DES/HMI (1977) *Curriculum 11 to 16*. London: DES.

DES/HMI (1979) *Aspects of Secondary Education in England*. London: HMSO.

DES/HMI (1980) *A View of the Curriculum*. London: HMSO.

DEPARTMENT OF EMPLOYMENT (1981) *A New Training Initiative: a programme for action*. London: HMSO.

DEVLIN, P. A. (1965) *The Enforcement of Morals*. Oxford: Oxford University Press.

DEVON COUNTY COUNCIL (1978) *Records 5 to 16: A Handbook of Guidance*. Exeter: Devon County Council.

DEVON COUNTY COUNCIL (1982) *Personal, Social and Moral Education*. Exeter: Devon Education Department.

DEWEY, J. (1916) *Democracy and Education*. London: Macmillan

DICKENS, F. and STEADMAN, R. (1967) *Fly away Peter*. Durham: Dobson

DIXON, B. (1977) *Catching them Young. Vol 1: Sex, Race, and Class in Children's Fiction*. London: Pluto Press.

DOWNIE, R. S. and TELFER, E. (1969) *Respect for Persons*. London: Allen and Unwin.

DOWNIE, R. S. and TELFER, E. (1980) *Caring and Curing*. London: Methuen.

D'ZURILLA, T. J. and GOLDFRIED, M. R. (1971) 'Problem-solving and behaviour modification', *Journal of Abnormal Psychology* 78.

ELLIOTT, J. (1981) 'How do parents judge schools?' in ELLIOTT, J., BRIDGES, D., EBBUTT, D., GIBSON, R., and NIAS, J. *School Accountability*. London: Grant McIntyre.

ELLIOTT, J. and MACDONALD, B. (eds) (1975) *People in Classrooms*. Norwich: CARE Occasional Publications Number 2.

ELLIS, R. and WHITTINGTON, D. (1981) *A Guide to Social Skill Training*. London: Croom Helm.

EVANS, D. (1982) 'The family of Mr Men' in *Children's Literature in Education*, 13 (3).

EVANS, D. (1983) 'Individual differences and autonomy in personal, social and moral education' in *Educational Analysis* 5 (1).

FELDMAN, M. (1981) 'Vocational education in an era of supply side economic policy' in GREENWOOD, K. B. (ed.) *Contemporary Challenges for Vocational Education*. Arlington, Virginia: 1982 Yearbook of the American Vocational Association.

FENTON, E. and KOHLBERG, L. (1976a) *Teacher Training in Values Education: A Workshop*. New York: Guidance Associates.

FENTON, E. and KOHLBERG, L. (1976b) *Universal Values in American History*. New York: Guidance Associates.

FENTON, E. and KOHLBERG, L. (1976c) *Values in a Democracy*. New York: Guidance Associates.

FLAVELL, J. H. (1974) 'The development of inference about others' in MISCHELL, T. (ed.) *Understanding Other Persons*. Oxford: Basil Blackwell.

FLETCHER, R. (1980) 'The Sutton Centre Profile' in BURGESS, T. and ADAMS, E. *Outcomes of Education*. London: Macmillan.

FROMM, E. (1942) *The Fear of Freedom*. London: Routledge and Kegan Paul.

FEU (1978) *Experience, Reflection, Learning*. London: DES.

FEU (1979) *A Basis for Choice*. London: DES.

FEU (1980a) *Developing social and life skills*. London: DES.

FEU (1980b) *Beyond coping*. London: DES.

FEU (1982a) *Tutoring*. London: DES.

FEU (1982b) *Profiles*. London: DES.

FEU (1984) *Common Core – Teaching and Learning*. London: DES.

GARBARINO, J. and BRONFENBRENNER, U. (1976) 'The socialisation of moral judgment and behaviour in cross-cultural perspective' in LICKONA, T. (ed.) *Moral development and behaviour*. New York: Holt, Rinehart and Winston.

GILLIGAN, C. (1982) *In a different voice: Psychological Theory and Women's Development*. Cambridge, Mass.: Harvard University Press.

GLEESON, D. and WHITTY, G. (1976) *Development in Social Studies Teaching*. London: Open Books.

GOODALL, O. (1983) 'Promoting social qualities in the primary school', *Educational Analysis* 5 (1).

GOODALL, O., BEALE, M., BELESCHENKO, A. and MUCHISON, P. (1983) *Developing Social Awareness in Young Children*. University of Exeter School of Education, Workbook Series 4.

GOW, R. M. (1980) *Yes, Virginia, There is Right and Wrong*. Toronto, Canada: Wiley and Sons.

GREENSTEIN, F. I. (1965) *Children and Politics*. New Haven, CT: Yale University Press.

HAMBLIN, D. (1974) *The Teacher and Counselling*. Oxford: Basil Blackwell.

HAMBLIN, D. H. (1978) *The Teacher and Pastoral Care*. Oxford: Basil Blackwell.

HANSARD SOCIETY (1974–77) *Programme for Political Education*. London: Hansard Society.

HARE, R. M. (1952) *The Language of Morals*. Oxford: Oxford University Press.

HARE, R. M. (1963) *Freedom and Reason*. Oxford: Oxford University Press.

HARE, R. M. (1973) 'Language and moral education' in LANGFORD, S. G. and O'CONNOR, D. J. (eds) *New Essays in the Philosophy of Education*. London: Routledge and Kegan Paul.

HARE, R. M. (1981) *Moral Thinking: its levels, method, and point*. Oxford: Oxford University Press.

HARGIE, O., SAUNDERS, C. and DICKSON, D. (1981) *Social Skills in Interpersonal Communication*. London: Croom Helm.

HARGREAVES, D. (1982) *The Challenge for the Comprehensive School*. London: Routledge and Kegan Paul.

HARTSHORNE, H. and MAY, M. A. (1928) *Studies in the Nature of Character*. New York: Macmillan.

HAYES, J. and HOPSON, B. (1971) *Careers Guidance: The Role of the School in Vocational Development*. London: Heinemann.

HEATER, D. B. and GILLESPIE, J. A. (1981) *Political Education in Flux*. London: Sage.

HEMMING, J. (1949) *The Teaching of Social Studies in Secondary Schools*. Harlow: Longman.

HERSH, R. H., PAOLITTO, D. P. and REIMER, J. (1979) *Promoting Moral Growth: from Piaget to Kohlberg*. New York: Longman.

HICKS, D. W. (1981) *Minorities: A Teacher's Resource Book for the Multiethnic Curriculum*. London: Heinemann.

HICKS, D. (1981) *Minorities: A Teacher's Resource Book for the Multiethnic Curriculum*. London: Heinemann.

HILDICK, W. (1970) *Children and Fiction*. London: Evans.

HIRST, P. H. (1965) 'Morals, Religion, and the Maintained School', *British Journal of Educational Studies* 14.

HIRST, P. H. (1974) *Moral Education in a Secular Society*. London: University of London Press Ltd.

HOFFMAN, M. (1975) 'Developmental Synthesis of Affect and Cognitive and Its Implications for altruistic motivation', *Developmental Psychology* 11 (5).

HOLT, J. (1964) *How Children Fail*. London: Pitman.

HOPSON, B. and HOUGH, P. (1973) *Exercises in Personal and Career Development.* Cambridge: CRAC.

HOPSON, B. and SCALLY, M. (1979) *Lifeskills Teaching Programmes*, Numbers 1 and 2. Leeds: Lifeskills Associates.

HOPSON, B. and SCALLY, M. (1981) *Lifeskills Teaching.* Maidenhead: McGraw Hill.

HOUSE OF COMMONS HOME AFFAIRS COMMITTEE (1981) *Racial Disadvantage.* London: HMSO.

HOWDEN, R. and DOWSON, H. (1973) *Practical Guidance in Schools: Educational and Vocational Guidance as an Integral Part of the School Curriculum.* London: Careers Consultants.

HULL, J. (ed.) (1982) *New Directions in Religious Education.* London: Falmer Press.

HUMBLE, S. and SIMONS, H. (1978) *From Council to Classroom: An Evaluation of the Diffusion of the Humanities Curriculum Project.* London: Macmillan.

HUSBAND, C. (ed.) (1982) *'Race' in Britain.* London: Hutchinson.

JACKSON, P. W. (1968) *Life in Classrooms.* New York: Holt, Rinehart and Winston.

JAMES, A. and JEFFCOATE, R. (1981) *The School in the Multicultural Society.* London: Harper and Row.

JAMIESON, I. and LIGHTFOOT, M. (1982) *Schools and Industry*, Schools Council Working Paper 73. London: Methuen.

JENKINS, D. (1976) 'Man: a course of study', Units 14–15 Part 3 in Open University Course E 203, *Curriculum Design and Development.* Milton Keynes: The Open University Press.

JONES, E. M. (1983) 'The uses employers make of examination results and other tests for selection and employment.' Unpublished report: Jones, J., School of Education University of Reading.

KANT, I. (1785) *Fundamental Principles of the Metaphysic of Morals*, translated by ABBOTT, T. K. (6th ed. 1909). London: Longman.

KAY, B. (1975) 'Monitoring school performance', *Trends in Education* July.

KAY, W. (revised ed., 1970) *Moral Development: a psychological study of moral growth from childhood to adolescence.* London: Allen and Unwin.

KAY, W. (1975) *Moral Education: a sociological study of the influence of society, home and school.* London: Allen and Unwin.

KELLY, A. (1981) *The Missing Half: Girls and Science Education.* Manchester: Manchester University Press.

KITWOOD, T. (1980) *Disclosures to a Stranger: adolescent values in an advanced industrial society.* London: Routledge and Kegan Paul.

KOHLBERG, L. (1971a) 'Stages of moral development as a basis for moral education' in BECK, C., CRITTENDON, B. and SULLIVAN, E. (eds) *Moral education interdisciplinary approaches.* Toronto: University of Toronto Press.

KOHLBERG, L. (1971b) 'From "is" to "ought": how to commit the naturalistic fallacy and get away with it in the study of moral development' in MISCHEL, T. (ed.) *Cognitive Development and Epistemology*. New York: Academic Press.

KOHLBERG, L. (1976) 'Moral stages and moralization: the cognitive developmental approach' in LICKONA, T. (ed.) *Moral Development and Behaviour: theory, research and social issues*. New York: Holt, Rinehart and Winston.

KOHLBERG, L. (1981) *Essays on Moral Development: Vol I The philosophy of moral development*. San Francisco, Calif.: Harper and Row.

KOHLBERG, L. (1982) 'Recent work in moral education' in WARD, L. O. (1982) *The Ethical Dimension of the School Curriculum*. Swansea: Pineridge Press.

KOHLBERG, L. (1983) *Essays on moral Development: Vol II The psychology of moral development*. San Francisco, Calif.: Harper and Row.

KRATHWOHL, D., BLOOM, B. and MASIA, B. (1964) *Taxonomy of Educational Objectives: Vol 2 Affective domain*. London: Longman.

KUHMERKER, L. (1981) 'Editorial', *Moral Education Forum* (1981, Summer).

LANGFORD, S. G. (1973) 'The Concept of Education' in LANGFORD, S. G. and O'CONNOR, D. J. (eds) *New Essays in the Philosophy of Education*. London: Routledge and Kegan Paul.

LAW, B. and WATTS, A. G. (1977) *Schools, Careers and Community: a study of some approaches to careers education in schools*. London: CIO Publishing.

LAWTON, D. and DUFOUR, B. (1973) *The New Social Studies*. London: Heinemann.

LEE, N. (1974) 'Concealed values in economics teaching' in WHITEHEAD, D. *Curriculum Development in Economics*. London: Heinemann.

LIGHT, P. (1980) *The Development of Social Sensitivity*. Cambridge: Cambridge University Press.

LITTLE, A. and WILLEY, R. (1981) *Multi-ethnic Education: the way forward* London: Schools Council.

LOEVINGER, J. (1976) *Ego Development*. San Francisco, Calif.: Jossey-Bass.

MACDONALD, B. (ed.) (1969) 'The experience of innovation' in *Towards Judgment II*. Norwich: CARE Occasional Publications Number 6.

MCINTOSH, P. (1974) *Fair Play: Ethics in sport and education*. London: Heinemann.

MACKIE, J. L. (1977) *Ethics: Inventing right and wrong*. Harmondsworth: Penguin.

MCLAUGHLIN, T. H. (1983) 'The pastoral curriculum: concept and principle', *Educational Analysis 5* (3).

MCPHAIL, P. (1982) *Social and Moral Education*. Oxford: Basil Blackwell.

MCPHAIL, P., MIDDLETON, D. and INGRAM, D. (1978) *Startline: Moral*

Education in the Middle Years. Schools Council Project *Moral Education 8 to 13*. Harlow: Longman.

MCPHAIL, P., UNGOED-THOMAS, J. R. and CHAPMAN, H. (1972), *Moral Education in the Secondary School*. Harlow: Longman.

MSC (1980) *Instructional Guide to Social and Life Skills*. London: MSC.

MSC (1981) *A New Training Initiative: a consultative document*. London: MSC.

MSC (1981) *A New Training Initiative: an agenda for action*. London: MSC.

MSC/FEU (1982) *A New Training Initiative: joint statement*. London: MSC.

MARCH, P. and SMITH, M. (1977 republished) *Your choice at 15+*. Cambridge: CRAC.

MARLAND, M. (1974) *Pastoral Care*. London: Heinemann.

MARLAND, M. (1980) 'The pastoral curriculum' in BEST, R., JARVIS, C. and RIBBINS, P. (eds) *Perspectives on Pastoral Care*. London: Heinemann.

MATHEWS, J. C. (1974) 'The assessment of attitudes' in MACINTOSH, H. G. (ed.) *Techniques and Problems of Assessment*. London: Edward Arnold.

MEAD, G. H. (1934) *Mind, self and society*. Chicago, Ill.: University of Chicago Press.

MIDWINTER, E. (1972) 'Curriculum and the EPA school' in MIDWINTER, E. *Projections: an educational priority area at work*. London: Ward Lock.

MIDWINTER, E. (1975) *Education and the Community*. London: Allen and Unwin.

MILNER, D. (1975) *Children and Race*. Harmondsworth: Penguin. Reprinted (1983) *Children and Race: Ten Years On*. London: Ward Lock.

MOSHER, R. (1980) *Moral Education: a first generation of research and development*. New York: Praeger.

MUSGRAVE, P. W. (1982) 'Some social influences on moral education' in WARD, L. O. (ed.) *The Ethical Dimension of the School Curriculum*. Swansea: Pineridge Press.

NELSON, R. and LEACH, J. (1981) 'Increasing opportunities for entrepreneurs' in GREENWOOD, K. B. *Contemporary challenges for Vocational Educators*. Arlington, Virginia: 1982, Yearbook of the American Vocational Association.

NIBLETT, R. (1960) *Christian Education in a Secular Society*. Oxford: Oxford University Press.

OLIVER, D. W. (1976) *Education and Community: a radical critique of innovative schooling*. Berkeley, Calif.: McCutchan.

O'HARE, P. (1978) *Foundation of Religious Education*. Chicago, Ill.: Paulist Press.

PETERS, R. S. (1966) *Ethics and Education*. London: Allen and Unwin.

PETERS, R. S. (1970) 'Education and the educated man' in *Proceedings of the Philosophy of Education Society of Great Britain*, 4.

PETERS, R. S. (1971) 'Moral Development: a plea for pluralisation' in MISCHEL, T. (ed.) *Cognitive Development and Epistemology*. New York: Academic Press.

PETERS, R. S. (1974a) 'Personal understanding and personal relationships' in MISCHEL, T. (1974) *Understanding Other Persons*. Oxford: Blackwell.

PETERS, R. S. (1974b) *Psychology and Ethical Development*. London: Allen and Unwin.

PETERS, R. S. (1977) *Education and the Education of Teachers*. London: Routledge and Kegan Paul.

PETERS, R. S. (1978) 'The place of Kohlberg's theory in moral education' in *Journal of Moral Education* 7 (3), reprinted in PETERS, R. S. (1981) *Moral Development and Moral Education*. London: Allen and Unwin.

PETERS, R. S. (1981) *Moral Development and Moral Education*. London: Allen and Unwin.

PIAGET, J. (1926) *The Language and Thought of the Child*. London: Routledge and Kegan Paul.

PIAGET, J. (1932) *The Moral Judgment of the Child*. London: Routledge and Kegan Paul.

PLATO (Trans. 1970, Lee, H.) *The Republic*. Harmondsworth: Penguin.

PONTON, G. and GILL, P. (1983) *Introduction to Politics*. Oxford: Martin Robertson.

PORTER, A. (1979) 'The Programme for political education: a guide for beginners', *The Social Science Teacher*, 8 (3) February.

POTEET, J. A. (1973) *Behaviour Modification*. London: University of London Press Ltd.

POWER, C. and REIMER, J. (1978) 'Moral atmosphere' in DAMON, W. *New Direction for Child Development and Moral Development*. San Francisco, Calif.: Jossey-Bass.

PRATLEY, B. (1982) 'Profiles in Practice', FEU Report *Profiles*.

PRING, R. A. (1980) 'Monitoring performance: reflections on the Assessment of Performance Unit' in LACEY, C. and LAWTON, D. (eds) *Issues in Evaluation and Accountability*. London: Methuen.

PRING, R. A. (1981) 'Behaviour modification: some reservations', *Perspectives 5*. Exeter: University of Exeter School of Education.

PRING, R. A. (1982) 'National assessment of social studies'. Unpublished paper, available from author.

PRING, R. A. (1983) *Privatisation*. London: RICE.

RAMPTON REPORT (1981) *West Indian Children in our Schools*. London: HMSO.

RATH, L. E. (1966) *Values and Teaching*. Wembley: Merrill.

RAWLS, J. (1977) *A Theory of Justice*. Oxford: Oxford University Press.

REID, L. A. (1969) *Meaning in the Arts*. London: Allen and Unwin.

RENNIE, J., LUNZER, E. A. and WILLIAMS, W. T. (1974) *Social Education:*

An Experiment in Four Secondary Schools, Schools Council Working Paper 51. London: Evans/Methuen.

RICHARDS, J. RADCLIFFE (1980) *The Sceptical Feminist*. London: Routledge and Kegan Paul.

ROSS, M. (1975) *Arts and the Adolescent*, Schools Council Working Paper 54. London: Evans.

THE RUNNYMEDE TRUST AND THE RADICAL STATISTICS RACE GROUP (1980) *Britain's Black Population*. London: Heinemann.

RUDDUCK, J. (1972) 'Man: a course of study', *Cambridge Journal of Education*, 2 (2).

RUTTER, M., MAUGHAN, B., MORTIMORE, P. and OUSTON, J. (1979) *Fifteen Thousand Hours*. London: Open Books.

SCHARF, P. (1978) *Moral Education*. David, California: Responsible Action.

SCHOFIELD, W. N. (1981) *Assessment of Personal and Social Development: a review of the literature*. London: DES.

SCHOOLS COUNCIL (1981) *The Practical Curriculum*. London: Methuen.

SCHOOLS COUNCIL/NUFFIELD HUMANITIES PROJECT (1970) *The Humanities Project – an introduction*. London: Heinemann.

SCRIMSHAW, P. (1981) *Community Service, Social Education and the Curriculum*. London: Hodder and Stoughton.

SECORD, P. F. and PEEVERS, B. H. (1974) 'The development and attribution of person concepts' in MISCHEL, T. (ed.) *Understanding Other Persons*. Oxford: Basil Blackwell.

SELMAN, R. L. (1976) 'Social Cognitive Understanding: a guide to educational and clinical practice' in LICKONA, T. (ed.) *Moral Development and Behaviour*. New York: Holt, Rinehart and Winston.

SIMNER, M. L. (1971) 'Newborn's response to the cry of another infant', *Developmental Psychology* 5.

SIMON, S. B. (1972) *Values Clarification: a handbook* New York: Hart.

SMITH, M. and MARCH, P. (1981) *Your choice at 17+*. Cambridge: CRAC.

SMITH, M. and MATTHEWS, V. (1980) *Your choice at 13+*. Cambridge: CRAC.

SPENDER, D. (1982) *Invisible Women: The Schooling Scandal*. London: Writers and Readers.

SPIVACK, G. and SHURE, M. B. (1974) *Social Adjustment of Young Children*. San Francisco, Calif.: Jossey-Bass.

STANSBURY, D. (1976) *Record of Personal Experience, Qualities and Qualifications*. South Brent: RPE Publications.

STANSBURY, D. (1980) 'The record of personal experience' in BURGESS, T. and ADAMS, E. (eds) *Outcomes of Education*. London: Macmillan.

STENHOUSE, L., VERMA, G. K., WILD, R. D. and NIXON, J. (1982) *Teaching About Race Relations: problems and effects*. London: Routledge and Kegan Paul.

STOATE, P. (1983) 'Curriculum development in personal and social education: the practice and the problems', *Educational Analysis* 5 (1).

STONE, M. (1981) *The Education of the Black Child*. London: Collins/Fontana.

STRADLING, R. (1978) 'Political education in the 11 to 16 curriculum', *Cambridge Journal of Education* 8.

STRAUGHAN, R. (1982) *Can We Teach Children to be Good?* London: Allen and Unwin.

STROM, M. S. (1981) 'Facing history and ourselves: integrating a holocaust unit into the curriculum' in *Moral Education Forum* (Summer).

STROM, M. S. and PARSONS, W. (1982) *Facing History and Ourselves: Holocaust and Human Behaviour*. Waterdown, Mass.: Intentional Education.

SUGARMAN, B. (1973) *The School and Moral Development*. London: Croom Helm.

SWALES, T. (1979) *Record of Personal Achievement: an independent evaluation of the Swindon RPA scheme*, Pamphlet 16. London: Schools Council.

TAWNEY, R. H. (1938) *Equality*. London: Allen and Unwin.

TAYLOR, M. J. (1981) *Caught Between*. Windsor: NFER-Nelson.

THACKER, J. (1982) *Steps to Success: a teacher's manual*. Windsor: NFER-Nelson.

THACKER, J. (1983) 'Interpersonal Problem-Solving Training: the underlying models and their application in programmes to prevent and to treat psychological disturbance', *Educational Analysis* 5 (1).

TOMLINSON, P. (1975) 'Political Education: Cognitive Developmental Perspectives from moral education', *Oxford Review of Education I* (3).

UNGOED-THOMAS, J. R. (1972) *Our School*. London: Longman.

UNGOED-THOMAS, J. R. (1978) *The Moral Situation of Children*. London: Macmillan.

VERMA, G. K. (ed.) (1980) 'The impact of innovation' in *Towards Judgment I*. Norwich: CARE Occasional Publications 9.

WARD, K. (1983) 'Is autonomy an educational ideal?' in *Educational Analysis*, 5 (1).

WARD, L. O. (1975) 'History and humanity's teacher?', *Journal of Moral Education*, 4 (2).

WARD, L. O. (ed.) (1983) *The Ethical Dimension of the School Curriculum*. Swansea: Pineridge Press.

WARNOCK, G. (1966) *Contemporary Moral Philosophy*. London: Macmillan.

WASSERMAN, E. R. (1976) 'Implementing Kohlberg's "Just Community Concept" in an Alternative High School' in *Social Education* 20 (4).

WASSERMAN, E. and GARROD, A. (1983) 'Application of Kohlberg's theory to curricula and democratic schools', *Educational Analysis* 5 (1).

WATTS, A. G. (1978) 'The implications of school leaver unemployment for careers education in schools', *Journal of Curriculum Studies*, 10 (3).

WATTS, A. G. (1980) 'Pastoral care and careers education' in BEST, R., JARVIS, C. and RIBBINS, P. *Perspective on Pastoral Care.* London: Heinemann.

WATTS, A. G., SUPER, D. E. and KIDD, J. M. (1981) *Career Development in Britain.* Cambridge: CRAC.

WATTS, J. (ed.) (1977) *The Countesthorpe Experience.* London: Allen and Unwin.

WEINREICH-HASTE, H. (1983) 'Developmental moral theory, with special reference to Kohlberg' in *Educational Analysis* 5 (1).

WHELAN, E. and SPEAKE, B. (1979) *Learning to Cope.* London: Souvenir Press.

WILKINSON, J. and CANTER, S. (1982) *Social Skills Training Manual.* Toronto, Canada: Wiley.

WILLEY, B. (1964) *The English Moralists.* London: Chatto and Windus.

WILLEY, R. (1982) *Teaching in Multicultural Britain.* Harlow: Longman Resources Unit.

WILLIAMS, T. and WILLIAMS, N. (1981) 'Personal and social development in the curriculum'. Schools Council Project *Health Education 13 to 18.*

WILLIS, P. (1977) *Learning to Labour.* Farnborough: Saxon House.

WILSON, J. (1961) *Reason and Morals.* Cambridge: Cambridge University Press.

WILSON, J. (1969) *Moral Education and the Curriculum.* London: Pergamon Press.

WILSON, J. (1972) *Practical Methods of Moral Education.* London: Heinemann.

WILSON, J. (1973) *A Teacher's Guide to Moral Education.* London: Chapman.

WILSON, J. (1982) 'First steps in moral education' in WARD, L. O. *The ethical dimension of the school curriculum.* Swansea: Pineridge Press.

WILSON, J., WILLIAMS, N. and SUGARMAN, B. (1967) *An Introduction to Moral Education.* Harmondsworth: Penguin.

WITKIN, R. W. (1974) *The Intelligence of Feeling.* London: Heinemann.

WOMEN'S NATIONAL COMMISSION (1983) *Secondary Education: report by an ad hoc working group.* WNC Government Offices, Great George Street, London SW1P 3AQ.

WRIGHT, D. (1971) *The Psychology of Moral Behaviour.* Harmondsworth: Penguin.

WRIGHT, D. (1982) 'Piaget's theory of practical morality' in *British Journal of Psychology* 73.

Index